Chinese Takeout Recipes

Recipes Inspired by Chinese Takeout That You Can Make at Home
(2022 Guide for Beginners)

Jia Nianzu

TABLE OF CONTENTS

INTRODUCTION

Takeout Chinese food has been around for a long time. It's tasty, inexpensive, and accessible at any time. It is served in a cleverly constructed and well-known cardboard box.

Surprisingly, most meals on a takeaway menu were formerly thought to be weird by the Chinese themselves. The fortune cookie, for example, is a product of the United States. Other meals supposed to be truly Chinese, such as fried rice and sweet-and-sour pork, are American.

A LITTLE HISTORICAL BACKGROUND

The majority of Chinese restaurants as we know them now offer Cantonese cuisine. Cantonese businessmen and tourists are credited with introducing Chinese food to the Western world. The earliest Chinese restaurants in the United States were the "chow chows" of 19th century California, which catered to the Cantonese workers who constructed the transcontinental rails. After being met with hostility at first, the ambitious entrepreneurs altered their recipes to suit American tastes. Some questioned its legitimacy, while others came to embrace its "Americanness." After WWII, Chinese restaurants continued to diversify and include American elements.

As immigration regulations grew more lenient, additional influences from Shanghai, Hunan, and Sichuan entered the nation.

By the 1970s, fusion had gained popularity, and even Chinese restaurants in Asia started to include non-traditional foods on their menus. The "chow chow" diners of the 1800s have gone a long way, with Chinese restaurants now outnumbering McDonald's.

Ingredients:

Chinese takeout dishes differ from their original counterparts in various ways. Chinese chefs don't waste anything and employ unusual ingredients like pig ears, chicken feet, and duck blood.

Takeout has been altered to suit the conservative westerner's preferences. Westernized Chinese cuisine is often seen to be fattier and lacking in flavors.

Authentic Chinese recipes emphasize veggies, rice, and soybeans, while Chinese takeout emphasizes them as side dishes.

Many western components, such as carrots, broccoli, onion, tomato, and dairy, have been employed in Americanized cuisine. Fruit canned in cans, such as pineapple, and sweet caramelized sauces are "all-American." Takeout offers a restricted selection of seafood options in comparison to the extensive selection offered in traditional Chinese cuisine. Regardless of these distinctions, Chinese takeaway is unquestionably popular, and it has come full circle, gaining favor even in the East.

Here are some common elements included in both traditional and Chinese takeout cuisines.

The soy sauce

Fermented soybeans are used to make light soy sauce, dark soy sauce, and standard soy sauce. Light soy sauce has a lighter hue but a higher saltiness. The dark soy sauce has been fermented for a longer period. It's less salty, a little sweeter, and has a deep caramel hue. Regular soy sauce falls somewhere in the middle between light and dark sauces.

Oil for Cooking

Deep frying is not often utilized in Chinese food, although numerous oils are. For enhanced scent, peanut oil is employed. Both corn and soy oil may be utilized. Pregnant ladies seek walnut oil for its nutritious benefits. Sesame oil is used to flavor meals rather than to cook them, and it is often poured over them before serving.

Fresh ginger, garlic, and scallions (spring onions) are utilized in a variety of ways, including whole, crushed, grated, or diced. They are used for flavoring and removing "fishiness," as well as for therapeutic purposes.

Powdered Five-Spice

A flavorful blend of well-known spices. It has fennel, peppercorns, star anise, cinnamon, and cloves in it.

Vinegar of rice

This is what is often used in Chinese cooking. It is available in either white or black. It gives Asian cuisine a unique taste.

Sauce with Oysters

Oysters and soy sauce combine to make a rich, thick brown sauce. It provides taste to a variety of meals.

Cornstarch

It is often combined with water and used to thicken sauces. To get the correct quantity of sauce to coat the components, a slurry of cornstarch and water is frequently added to the boiling ingredients. It's also utilized in the preparation of crispy coatings for fried meats, veggies, and seafood.

Salt

In Chinese cookery, salt is highly prized. It brings out the best in all tastes.

(This is why some physicians restrict patients who need to limit their salt intake from eating Chinese cuisine.)

Wine made with rice

Rice wine, often known as Shaoxing, is used in marinating and braising. It has a taste that is akin to dry sherry. When stir-frying, it is applied by pouring around the lip of the pan for faster alcohol dispersion and improved taste. It is also used with soy sauce and spices to make sauces and marinades. Dry sherry and sake are acceptable substitutes. If you're using mirin, use 12 teaspoons of sugar for every tablespoon of mirin.

Methods of Cooking

Chinese food employs a variety of cooking methods.

Chinese chefs strive to retain food's freshness, color, nutrition, and texture. Frying is used more often in takeout meals. Despite being done in a wok, frying is not a common cooking technique in real Chinese food. Breading is another technique with American origins. Americanized foods, on the other hand, are developing, and westerners are getting more daring in their palates. Many Chinese restaurants are no longer afraid to use traditional cooking techniques and provide more genuine cuisine.

Stir-Fry

This cooking technique gained popularity in America because it is fast, low-fat, and nutrient-rich. It entails marinating thinly sliced meat (often pre-cooked) and vegetables in a soy sauce-based sauce. These are fried in a super-hot wok with very little oil and a lot of stirring. As a consequence, you get a hot, fresh meal with crisp and flavorful components. Larger works are favored for even heat distribution and improved texture and taste. The secret to successful stir-frying is, to begin with, a very hot wok before adding oil.

Steaming

This time, space, and fuel-saving cooking technique exemplifies Chinese resourcefulness and invention. The steamer is constructed of bamboo baskets piled one on top of the other in about three layers.

Several types of food may be cooked at the same time in a slow-boiling pot of water. Dim sum, such as buns or dumplings, pancakes, and fish, are popular steamed foods.

Red Stewing Sauce

The term is derived from the rich, brown color of the meals produced by this cooking process. Unlike stir-fry, which needs the least amount of cooking time, this approach takes many hours to prepare. Meats are often seared first before being simmered with soy sauce, rice wine, and traditional seasonings until soft and flavorful.

Roasting

Ovens are used for roasting large amounts of meat, as well as entire chickens and ducks. These are then finely sliced or diced and served with a rich sauce or gravy.

Boiling

Commonly used for vegetables that are swiftly cooked, drained, and then served with a rich sauce. This technique is also used to prepare noodles and soups.

Poaching

his technique is often used to prepare fish. To add taste, a nice broth is added.

frying in hot oil

This technique is thought to be more common in Americanized dishes than in traditional cookery. The end product is a crisp and appetizing dinner.

9

Recipes for Chinese Takeout

The fundamental tools are similar to those found in any conventional kitchen. Here are some great tools for making your cooking more enjoyable and genuine.

Wok

What is Chinese cookery if not cooked in a wok? A wok is a multi-purpose tool that may be used for stir-frying, boiling, steaming, and deep-frying. Its rounded bottom allows for more effective heat usage. Chefs favor huge woks for more effective heat dispersion and better texture and taste outcomes.

Using a rice cooker

This is a fantastic ingredient for Chinese cookery. It eliminates the need to continually monitor the rice cooking in a clay pot and allows you to focus on other tasks. The rice cooker may also be used to boil and steam vegetables.

Steamer

Traditional steamers are made of layers of bamboo baskets, although newer variants might be made of metal. This is often used in dim sum and seafood dishes.

Cleaver

A huge knife for slicing, chopping, and cutting. The flat side may be used to smash or crush garlic, ginger, and peppercorns.

Chopsticks

Chopsticks are a must-have for every Chinese chef. They may be used to pick up ingredients, loosen strands of noodles, mix, flip, and even measure powdered ingredients. Cooking chopsticks are made of bamboo or wood and are longer than conventional chopsticks.

Chinese shears

These are considerably easier and quicker to use than knives. They are suitable for meats, poultry, shellfish, vegetables, and herbs.

Strainer for spiders

This instrument is used for both scooping and straining. It features a web-like mesh and is great for freshly cooked noodles as well as deep-fried rolls, chicken, or seafood.

Now that we've gathered all of the necessary materials and equipment, it's time to get to work.

Recipes for Appetizers

Traditional Egg Rolls

Serving : 8-10 people

Time to Prepare: 10 minutes

Time to cook: 15-29 minutes

Marinade Ingredients

2 tbsp of soy sauce

2 tbsp of oyster sauce

1 teaspoon vinegar (rice)

3 minced garlic cloves

2 tablespoons minced fresh ginger 12 teaspoons brown sugar

To roll

1 pound pork ground

1 teaspoon cornstarch

two tbsp vegetable oil

2 cups shredded cabbage

1 medium peeled and shredded carrot

seasoned with salt & pepper

1 egg roll wrapper package

13

Deep-frying peanut oil

Directions

1. In a mixing bowl, combine all of the marinade ingredients and whisk thoroughly.

2. Stir in the ground pork and cornstarch. It's better to do this with clean or gloved hands.

3. Allow the mixture to marinate for 5 minutes.

4. Heat the vegetable oil in a wok over medium heat. Cook until the meat is no longer pink.

5. Cook until the cabbage and carrots are cooked thoroughly (about 2 minutes).

6. Season with salt and pepper to taste, then remove from fire.

7. Arrange one wrapper at a time in a diamond form on a clean surface or tray.

8. Place around 14 or 13 cups of the pork filling towards the bottom tip of the diamond, closest to you. If you put too much filling in the wrapper, it will break while it is cooking.

9. Fold the wrapper's bottom tip over the filling. Once, roll firmly.

10. Roll up to the top corner, folding the left and right corners inside.

11. To seal the roll, moisten the top corner with a little water or a mixture of water and cornstarch.

12. Continue until all of the filling or wrappers are gone.

13. Preheat the peanut oil in a wok over medium-high heat. When wooden chopsticks dipped in the oil emit small bubbles, the oil is ready.

14. Fry the rolls in batches until they are golden brown.

Do not overcrowd the rolls in the oil for more effective heating and crisp rolls.

15. Remove the rolls from the oil using a spider strainer or tongs and lay them on a plate lined with paper towels.

16. Serve immediately

Spring Rolls with Pork

25-50 people

Time to prepare: 30 minutes + 20 minutes marinating

Time to cook: 30 minutes

Ingredients

2 lbs ground pork

For the marinade

2 tbsp cornstarch and 2 tbsp rice wine vinegar

two tbsp rice wine

1 tsp. salt 1 tsp. ground black pepper

16

As a dipping sauce

2 teaspoons water

2 and a half tablespoons of sugar

4 teaspoons spicy sauce

6 tbsp of soy sauce

two tbsp rice vinegar

2 tablespoons rice wine

To fill

4 tbsp vegetable oil, split 10 cups cabbage, shredded 2 big carrots, shredded 3 garlic cloves, minced

10 dried shiitake mushrooms, rehydrated in boiling water, pressed and minced 1 teaspoon fresh ginger, peeled and grated 1 8-ounce can bamboo shoots, drained, squeezed, and shredded

1 cup chopped green onion

2 tbsp cornstarch

1 teaspoon granulated sugar

4 tbsp of soy sauce

2 tbsp. sesame oil

two tbsp rice wine

50 wrappers for spring rolls

frying oil

Pork Cooking Instructions

1. Combine the marinade ingredients in a large mixing dish. Mix in the meat well. Allow the mixture to sit for 15-20 minutes to marinate.

To make the dipping sauce

2. In a separate dish, mix the dipping sauce ingredients. Allow the flavors to blend before serving.

To make the filling

3. In a wok, heat 2 tablespoons of oil over medium heat. Quickly blanch the cabbage in the oil for around 2 minutes. To prevent burning, adjust the heat as required. Remove the cabbage from the oil with a slotted spoon and place it on a dish to cool.

4. Cook the carrots in the same manner, using whatever oil is left in the pan (you may need to add another tablespoon if necessary).

Using a slotted spoon, remove the carrots from the oil and put them aside to cool.

5. Heat the remaining oil in the wok. Cook until the marinated pork is browned and all of the liquid has been reduced.

6. Cook for another 2-3 minutes after adding the garlic and ginger.

Don't let the garlic burn.

7. Add the bamboo and mushrooms and cook for 3-5 minutes, or until heated through.

8. Remove the wok from the heat and place it on a cooling rack to cool.

9. Once the pork mixture has cooled, stir in the cabbage and carrots, as well as the mushrooms, green onion, cornstarch, sugar, soy sauce, sesame oil, and rice wine. Thoroughly combine.

To prepare the rolls

10. Lay a wrapper down on a clean surface. Place it so that it forms a diamond.

11. Place around 14-13 cups of filling on the wrapper, 1 12 to 2 inches from the bottom corner.

12. Fold the bottom corner over the filling and wrap it up tightly once.

13. Fold in the right and left corners and roll up to the top corner.

14. Moisten the top corner with water to aid in the sealing of the roll. You may also use a water-cornstarch mixture as an adhesive to help it cling better.

15. Continue until the filling is depleted. You should be able to get approximately 50 rolls out of this recipe.

16. Heat the cooking or peanut oil in a wok or frying pan over medium heat, approximately 2 inches deep.

17. Deep-fry the rolls till golden brown. Do not cook too many rolls at once for efficient frying and crisp rolls; fry them in batches.

18. Remove the completed rolls using a spider strainer and lay them on a plate coated with paper towels.

19. Serve immediately with the dipping sauce. Before serving, the rolls may be halved diagonally.

Spring Rolls with vegetables

50 servings

Time to prepare: 45 minutes

Time to cook: 30 minutes

Ingredients :

1 ½ cup bean sprouts 8 shiitake mushrooms

1 tbsp sesame seed oil

3 trimmed and sliced green onions

3 minced garlic cloves

1 teaspoon freshly grated ginger

2 medium shredded carrots 2 12 cups shredded green cabbage 8 ounces canned bamboo shoots, drained and thinly sliced

2 tbsp soy sauce (low sodium)

2 tbsp peanut oil (or your preferred oil)

1 egg, beaten with 2 tablespoons of water 50 spring roll wrappers, thawed

frying oil

Directions

1. Drain and wash the bean sprouts. Set things aside for now.

2. Wash and wipe dry the mushrooms. Finely julienne them.

3. In a skillet or wok, heat 1 tablespoon sesame oil over medium-high heat. Combine the green onions, garlic, and ginger in a mixing bowl.

For approximately 1 minute, stir-fry.

4. Stir in the rest of the veggies. Cook for 3-4 minutes, or until the vegetables are soft.

5. Combine the soy sauce and peanut oil in a mixing bowl. Stir everything together well. Cook for 1 minute longer before removing from the heat.

6. Strain the filling to remove the majority of the cooking juices. In a bowl, combine the filling ingredients.

7. Open the spring roll packet and lay all but one wrapper beneath a clean, moist dishtowel to prevent the wrappers from drying out.

8. Place your wrapper on a flat surface with one corner pointing towards you.

9. Spread a heaping spoonful of filling on the bottom of the wrapper, approximately two inches above the corner point.

10. Fold the bottom section of the wrapper over the filling, then fold the sides over the filling, creating an envelope with a long flap.

11. Roll the spring roll away from you until it's about two inches from the top, then brush the top edges with your egg wash, finish the roll, and repeat.

12. Wipe off the final rolls with a clean, damp dishtowel.

13. When you've finished all of your rolls, line a plate with paper towels.

14. Pour half a cup of oil into a heavy saucepan for cooking. Warm the oil in a medium saucepan over medium heat until it reaches 350oF. A wok or a deep fryer may also be used. Deep-fried spring rolls till golden brown, approximately 1-2 minutes on each side.

15. Before serving, place spring rolls on a dish lined with paper towels to absorb any extra oil.

16. Serve with your preferred dipping sauce.

Wontons Fried

10-12 people

Time to prepare: 12 hours

Time to cook: 20 minutes

Ingredients :

1 bag of ingredients (about 50 pieces) wrappers for wontons

frying oil

To make the filling

24

1 pound pork ground

2 tablespoons finely chopped scallions

1 tbsp sesame oil

1 teaspoon soy sauce

1 tbsp rice wine

½ teaspoons of sugar

1 teaspoon of peanut oil

18 tsp ground white pepper

To make the dipping sauce

1 tbsp. water, 1 tbsp. sugar, and 12 tbsp. light soy sauce

1 tsp Worcestershire sauce

½ tsp rice vinegar

1 teaspoon sesame sccds, roasted

Instructions for Filling

1. Combine all of the filling ingredients and thoroughly combine with your hands or a food processor until the mixture is paste-like inconsistent.

To prepare the wontons

2. Prepare a baking sheet or tray by lining it with parchment paper.

3. Place a wrapper on a plate or clean surface, and fill with approximately a teaspoon of filling.

4. Dab a dab of water around the contents to moisten the wrapping. This will aid in the adhesion of the wrapper's sides.

5. Fold the paper into a rectangle or a triangle, pressing the corners together to seal. Bring the bottom corners of a rectangle together until they overlap, wet with water, and press to seal. Bring the side corners of a triangle together until they overlap and seal. Repeat until all of the filler has been used up. This recipe yields around 40-50 wontons.

6. Arrange the wontons on the prepared baking sheet, allowing space between them to prevent them from sticking.

7. To keep them, wrap them in plastic wrap and place them in the freezer. When frozen, they keep for 2 months.

As a dipping sauce

8. Make the sauce before frying the wontons so that the flavors can combine while the sauce sits.

9. In a mixing dish, combine all of the sauce ingredients.

to frying

10. In a wok or skillet, heat enough oil for frying over medium heat.

The oil should be at a depth of 2 to 3 inches.

11. Fry the wontons in batches, flipping them over if necessary or keeping them immersed to ensure even cooking.

12. Drain them on paper towels.

13. Toss with the dipping sauce and serve.

Dumplings

30-40 servings

Time to prepare: 2 hours

Time allotted: 2 hours and 15 minutes

Ingredients:

3 pounds cleaned bok choy

1 ½ lb. ground pork

⅔ cup of rice wine

½ CUP VEGAN OIL

3 tbsp sesame seed oil

1 teaspoon salt

3 tbsp of soy sauce

14 tsp white pepper

13 cup of water

3-4 dumpling wrappers

Sauce pourable

½ c. soy sauce

½ teaspoon rice vinegar

1 teaspoon spicy chili sauce

1 finely sliced green onion

Directions

1. Remove the bok choy's bottoms and blanch it in boiling water.

Transfer it to ice cold water right away. Drain, carefully squeeze out the water, and pat dry with paper towels. Place the bok choy in a large mixing bowl and coarsely chop it.

2. Stir in the ground pork, rice wine, vegetable oil, sesame oil, salt, soy sauce, white pepper, and water.

3. Prepare a baking sheet by lining it with parchment paper and setting it aside.

4. On a clean surface, place a wrapper and pour approximately a spoonful of filling into the middle.

5. Moisten the sides of the circle with water and fold it in half.

6. Seal the edges by pressing them together.

7. Fold the edges into a fan form (about 4 folds).

8. Arrange the dumplings on the baking sheet, not too close together so they don't cling.

9. To store, wrap in cling wrap and place in the freezer overnight. Place the frozen dumplings in another container or Ziploc bags and return to the freezer.

10. You may either boil or fry the dumplings. When prepared dumplings are boiled, they float to the top. To fry, deep fried till golden brown or pan cook until golden brown.

29

11. Toss with a dipping sauce of 12 cup soy sauce, 12 tablespoon rice vinegar, and a sprinkle of chili sauce. Mix in the green onions well.

Peanut-sauced dumplings

about 40 pieces.

Time to prepare: 1 hour 30 minutes.

Time to cook: 30 minutes.

Ingredients:

30

Dumplings

2 tablespoons vegetable oil

2 cloves garlic, minced

1 teaspoon fresh ginger, grated

3 green onions, sliced

1 ½ cups napa cabbage, shredded

4 tablespoons bamboo shoots, shredded

1 pound ground pork

2 tablespoons soya sauce

1 teaspoon salt

1 tablespoon rice wine vinegar

¼ teaspoon white pepper

2 tablespoons sesame oil

40-50 round dumpling wrappers

Egg wash for sealing (1 egg beaten with 1-2 tablespoons of water)

Peanut sauce

½ cup smooth organic peanut butter

1 cup water

1 tablespoon soy sauce

1 tablespoon hoisin sauce

1 teaspoon chili paste

1 pinch hot chili pepper flakes

Crushed peanuts and sliced green onions for garnish

Directions

<u>Dumplings</u>

1. In a wok, heat 2 tablespoons vegetable oil over medium-high heat. Mix in the garlic and ginger. Cook for 30 seconds.

Reduce the heat to medium-high and stir in the green onions, napa cabbage, and bamboo shoots. Sauté the veggies until they are soft. Remove from the fire and set aside for a few minutes to cool.

2. Combine the uncooked ground pork with the vegetable combination. Combine thoroughly.

Combine the soy sauce, salt, vinegar, white pepper, and sesame oil in a mixing bowl.

3. Spread 1–12 teaspoons of the pork filling on one side of the wrapper. Seal the dumplings by gently coating the edges

with egg wash and folding them over. To seal, softly press. If desired, make a pleat.

4. You may prepare the dumplings by steaming (which is preferred for superior taste) or boiling them.

5. When boiling, just add them to the saucepan after the water has begun to boil. Allow them to boil for 12 minutes.

6. Fill the bottom of a bamboo steamer with cabbage, bok choy, or big lettuce leaves if used. It will keep the dumplings from adhering to the bottom of the pan. Steam the dumplings for 15 minutes, making sure they don't touch.

Sauce with Peanuts

7. In a blender, combine all of the sauce ingredients and blend until smooth.

8. If required, add additional water to get the desired consistency.

9. Pour enough sauce over the dumplings to thoroughly cover them.

If desired, top with crushed peanuts and green onions.

Serve right away.

Please keep in mind that depending on the chili paste you choose, this sauce might be rather hot. It's a good idea to sample and adjust the spice level if necessary. You may begin by using just 14 teaspoons of chili paste and omitting the chili pepper flakes.

Then tweak to your taste.

Shrimp Toast

4 servings

Time to Prepare: 10 minutes

Time to cook: 5 minutes

Ingredients

8 ounces shrimp, cooked and peeled

2 cloves garlic, crushed

1 tablespoon soy sauce

34

1 teaspoon sesame oil

1 large egg

4 slices white bread, crusts removed

1 tablespoon sesame seeds, toasted

2 tablespoons vegetable oil

Sweet and sour sauce, to use as dip

Directions

1. Puree the shrimp and garlic in a blender or food processor.

2. Combine the soy sauce, sesame oil, and egg in a mixing bowl. Pulse or process for a few more seconds, or until the mixture is paste-like inconsistency.

3. Spread the paste over the pieces of bread.

4. Top with sesame seeds. Use a spatula or the back of a spoon to press the sesame seeds into the mixture.

5. In a pan over medium heat, heat the oil.

6. Cut the bread into tiny triangles and cook them spread side up for 3-4 minutes, or until golden brown.

7. Drain on a cooling rack or a paper towel-lined platter.

8. Toss with sweet and sour sauce and serve.

Spare Ribs with Garlic

4-6 people

Time to Prepare: 15 minutes

Time to cook: 45 minutes

Ingredients

Water for boiling ribs

4 pounds spareribs, cut apart

For sauce

1 ½ cups brown sugar

36

1 ½ cups water

5 cloves garlic

3 ½ tablespoons light soy sauce

1 tablespoon oyster sauce

1 ½ tablespoons dry mustard

Spring onions, chopped (for garnish

Directions

1. Fill a saucepan halfway with water and bring to a boil.

2. Add the spareribs and cook, covered, until the meat is soft (about 30 minutes).

3. Remove the ribs from the soup and set them aside to drain.

4. Combine the sauce ingredients in a separate saucepan or wok.

5. Bring to a slow boil before adding the spareribs.

6. Return to a boil and simmer for 10-15 minutes.

7. If preferred, garnish with chopped spring onion.

Meatballs Kon Tiki Bobo

6-8 people

Time to prepare: 30 minutes

Time to cook: 10 minutes

Ingredients

Meatball ingredients

1 pound ground pork

1 cup white breadcrumbs

½ teaspoon ground ginger

¼ cup white sugar

1 cloves garlic, minced

Salt and pepper

Oil for frying

Batter ingredients

1 ½ cups all-purpose flour

4 tablespoons white sugar

2 teaspoons baking soda

1 cup water

2 eggs

Directions

1. Combine all of the meatball ingredients in a mixing dish. Season with salt and pepper to taste.

2. Make meatballs of the same size, approximately 34 inches in diameter. Set things aside for now.

3. To make the batter, whisk together the flour, sugar, and baking soda. Season with salt and pepper to taste. Fill a small dish halfway with the flour mixture.

4. Combine the eggs and water in a separate shallow dish.

5. Roll each meatball in the flour mixture after dipping it in the egg mixture. Place the balls on a platter.

6. Heat the frying oil or use a deep fryer. Fry the meatballs for 5 minutes in batches. Drain the excess fat by placing them on a tray lined with paper towels

7. Serve with cocktail toothpicks and a sweet and sour or cherry sauce dipping sauce.

Soup Recipes

Egg Drop Soup

servings: 4

Time to prepare: 10 minutes.

Time to cook: 5 minutes.

40

Ingredients

For thickener

2 tablespoons cornstarch

3 tablespoons water

For soup

1 14-ounce can chicken broth

1 cup water

¼ teaspoon white pepper

½ teaspoon salt

2 large eggs, lightly beaten

1 stalk spring onion, chopped

Directions

1. Combine the water and cornstarch to make the thickening.

Set it aside after making a slurry of it.

2. Bring the broth and water to a boil in a saucepan.

3. Combine the pepper, salt, and thickener in a mixing bowl. Remove the soup from the heat as it starts to thicken.

41

4. Pour in the beaten egg and whisk it with a pair of chopsticks a few times to make egg "ribbons."

5. Cook for another 2 minutes, covered.

6. Garnish with spring onion and serve right away

Soup with Hot and Sour Sauce

10-12 people

Time to Prepare: 5 minutes

Time to cook: 25 minutes

Ingredients

42

For thickener

5 tablespoons cornstarch

5 tablespoons water

For soup

6 cups chicken broth

4 ounces chicken breast, sliced thinly

2 tablespoons soy sauce

½ cup dried shiitake mushrooms, soaked in hot water to rehydrate,

de-stemmed and sliced

1 15-ounce can peeled straw mushrooms

2 tablespoons garlic red chili paste

¾ teaspoon ground pepper

½ ounce dried black fungus (soak in water for an hour before using)

1 7-ounce can sliced bamboo shoots

1 7-ounce can sliced water chestnuts

1 15-ounce can baby sweet corn cobs

½ pound soft tofu, sliced into ¼-inch cubes

¼ cup rice vinegar

4 eggs, beaten

1 teaspoon sesame oil

Green onion, finely chopped (to garnish)

Directions

1. Combine the cornstarch and water. Make a slurry using the ingredients and leave it aside.

2. Bring the broth to a boil in a saucepan, then lower it to a simmer.

3. Combine the chicken, soy sauce, mushrooms, and chili paste in a mixing bowl.

Cook for 10 minutes.

4. Combine the pepper, fungus, bamboo shoots, water chestnuts, baby corn, and tofu in a mixing bowl. Simmer for 10 minutes more.

5. While stirring, add the thickener. Stir the soup until it starts to thicken.

6. Pour in the eggs in a narrow stream while continually stirring. Cook for 10 seconds before removing from the heat.

7. Add the sesame oil and mix well.

8. Garnish with chopped green onion and serve.

Soup with Wontons

4-6 people

Time to prepare: 2 hours

Time to cook: 30 minutes

<u>For wonton filling</u>

½ pound medium prawns (shelled, deveined)

½ pound ground pork

1 tablespoon shallots, finely chopped

¼ cup cilantro, finely chopped

2 green onion stalks, thinly sliced

1 teaspoon fish sauce

1 teaspoon sugar

2 teaspoons rice wine

For broth

1 cinnamon stick

1 tablespoon fennel

1 tablespoon coriander seeds

1 star anise

6 cups chicken broth

2 tablespoons fish sauce

1 teaspoon white sugar

½ cup cilantro leaves, for garnish

Green onion, for garnish

Chili sauce

Directions

1. Pat the prawns dry with paper towels and finely cut.

2. In a mixing bowl, combine all of the filling ingredients and well combine.

3. Lay a clean wonton wrapper on a clean surface.

4. Spoon roughly 1 spoonful of filling into the center of each wrapper.

Moisten the wrapper around the filling with a dab of water; this will assist the edges of the wrapper holding together.

5. Fold the paper into a rectangle or a triangle, pressing the corners together to seal. Bring the bottom corners of a rectangle together until they overlap, wet with water, and press to seal. Bring the side corners of a triangle together until they overlap, then seal. Repeat until the filling is depleted.

6. Arrange the wontons on a baking sheet lined with parchment paper. To avoid sticking, leave some space between the parts. Cover with plastic wrap and freeze for long-term storage (approximately 2 months).

7. Bring water to a boil in a kettle. Add the wontons in stages, stirring with chopsticks to prevent them from adhering to the pan.

After approximately 3 minutes, the wontons are done when they float to the top.

8. Arrange the wontons in serving dishes.

9. Tie a square piece of cheesecloth into a knot with the cinnamon stick, fennel, coriander, and star anise.

10. Bring the chicken stock to a boil before beginning to make the soup. Place the spice packet in the hot broth. Reduce the heat to a low simmer and cover the saucepan.

11. Remove the spice packet after 30 minutes of simmering.

12. Stir in the fish sauce and sugar, adjusting the quantities to taste.

13. Ladle the heated soup into the wonton-ready bowls.

14. Garnish with cilantro and green onions and serve with chili sauce on the side.

RECIPES FOR NOODLES AND RICE

Noodles from Singapore

Preparation Time: 20 minutes Servings: 2

Time to cook: 10 minutes

Ingredients

2 eggs, beaten

1 14-ounce pack rice stick noodles

8-12 shrimp, peeled and deveined

49

1 tablespoon vegetable oil

1 Chinese sausage, chopped

3 cups napa cabbage, shredded

½ red onion, sliced thinly

3 dried red chili peppers

1 carrot, julienned

1 ½ tablespoons curry powder

2 teaspoons salt

1 tablespoon rice wine

½ teaspoon sesame oil

½ tablespoon soy sauce

Pinch of white pepper

1 green onion, chopped

Directions

1. Make an omelet using the eggs. Set them aside after cutting them into strips.

2. Soak the noodles for 20 minutes in cold water. When you're prepared to start cooking, drain them.

3. Using paper towels, dry the shrimp and cut slits lengthwise, or "butterfly" them.

4. In a wok, heat the oil over high heat. Stir-fry the shrimp and sausage for approximately 10 seconds, or until the shrimp become orange.

5. Combine the cabbage, onion, chiles, and carrot in a mixing bowl. Continue to stir-fry for another 30 seconds.

6. Stir in the curry powder.

7. Keep the heat on high. While adding the drained noodles to the pan, tear them into 8-inch long strands.

8. Stir in the salt and wine. To keep the noodles from sticking to the bottom of the pan, continually mix and scrape.

9. Add the sesame oil, soy sauce, and white pepper after the noodles have become yellow from the curry. Mix for another 2 minutes.

10. Garnish with the omelet slices and green onion.

11. Serve while still hot.

Beef Chow Fun

Serves: 2-3

Preparation Time: 1 hour

 Cooking Time: 5 minutes

Ingredients

8 ounces flank steak, cut across the grain in strips

For the marinade

¼ teaspoon baking soda

1 teaspoon cornstarch

1 teaspoon soy sauce

1 teaspoon oil

For the rest of the dish

3 tablespoons oil, divided

1 thumb ginger, cut into thin slices

4 scallions, halved lengthwise and cut into 3-inch pieces

1 12-ounce pack fresh flat rice noodles, pre-cut

2 tablespoons rice wine

½ teaspoon sesame oil

2 tablespoons dark soy sauce

2 tablespoons regular soy sauce

⅛ teaspoon sugar

Salt and white pepper, to taste

4 ounces fresh mung bean sprouts

Directions

1. Combine the marinade ingredients and marinate the meat for 1 hour.

2. Preheat the wok until it is scorching hot. Sear the meat in 1 12 teaspoon oil until browned. Take the meat out of the pan and put it aside.

3. Cook the ginger in the remaining oil until aromatic.

4. Stir in the scallions and noodles, making sure they are uniformly distributed across the pan.

5. Stir-fry for approximately 15 seconds over high heat.

6. Pour the wine into the pan, spooning it over the rim.

7. Combine the sesame oil, soy sauces, sugar, and white pepper in a mixing bowl.

With a spatula, scrape the bottom of the pan and raise the noodles upwards to combine.

8. Cook, stirring constantly until the noodles are uniformly covered with sauce and cooked through.

9. Combine the meat and sprouts in a mixing bowl and sauté until the sprouts are tender and the beef is cooked through.

Chow Mein with Pork.

1 serving

Time to Prepare: 5 minutes

Time to cook: 20 minutes.

Ingredients:

For marinade

1 teaspoon rice wine

55

1 teaspoon soy sauce

Dash salt

For noodles

4 ounces lean pork, cut into thin strips

7 ounces Hong Kong noodles (chow mein noodles)

1 teaspoon vegetable oil, for noodles, divided

1 tablespoon peanut or vegetable oil, for stir-frying

Dash ground chili

½ small onion, minced

1 teaspoon ginger, chopped

1 tablespoon green onion, chopped

½ cup cabbage, shredded

1 small carrot, julienned

½ cup green beans, sliced

2 small red bell peppers, sliced into strips

½ teaspoon salt

2 tablespoons chicken stock

1-2 tablespoons tomato ketchup (or according to taste)

Direction

Combine the marinade ingredients in a mixing bowl. Allow the pork to stand for 5-10 minutes after adding it to the sauce.

To prepare the noodles

2. Preheat the steamer by filling it halfway with water and bringing it to a mild boil. To avoid sticking, coat the bottom of the steamer basket with oil.

3. Cook the noodles for around 2-3 minutes.

4. Place the noodles in a mixing basin and toss in 12 teaspoons of oil using chopsticks.

5. Return the noodles to the steaming basket and continue to simmer for another 2-3 minutes.

6. Place them in a basin and put them away.

To prepare the chow mein

7. Melt the butter in a wok over high heat. Stir-fry the pork in the peanut or vegetable oil until it is no longer pink.

8. Combine the ground chili, onion, ginger, and green onion in a mixing bowl. Fry until fragrant.

9. Cook for 1 minute, stirring frequently, after adding the cabbage, carrot, green beans, and bell pepper.

10. Stir in the salt and chicken stock and simmer until the liquid is gone.

11 Stir in the ketchup and noodles. Mix until properly combined and well hot.

Lo Mein with Chicken, Pork, and Shrimp

4 servings

Time to Prepare: 30 minutes

Time to cook: 20 minutes

Ingredients

58

2 cups chicken broth, divided

¼ cup rice wine

¼ cup soy sauce

4 teaspoons cornstarch

4 ounces lean pork, very finely sliced

4 ounces boneless skinless chicken breasts, cut into thin slices

2 teaspoons sesame oil

2-4 pieces shrimp, cleaned, shelled and deveined

3 cloves garlic, minced

½ teaspoon ground ginger

4 green onions, chopped, plus more for garnish

½ small can water chestnuts, chopped

2 cups cabbage, finely shredded

1 cup celery, thinly sliced

1 cup frozen green peas, thawed and drained

1 carrot, peeled and shredded

8 ounces thin or angel hair spaghetti, cooked and drained

Directions

1. Heat 12 cups of broth in a skillet.

2. Combine the wine, soy sauce, and cornstarch in a separate dish with the remaining liquid. Set aside after thoroughly mixing.

3. Bring the stock to a boil in the skillet. Boil the pork for 2 minutes after adding it to the pot. Cook until both the chicken and the vegetables are no longer pink in the middle.

4. Transfer the pork and chicken to a platter with a slotted spoon and set aside. Remove any remaining liquid from the skillet.

5. Heat the sesame oil in a pan over medium-high heat.

6. Cook the shrimp, garlic, and ginger until aromatic and the shrimp has turned orange.

7. Cook for 3 minutes, or until the green onion, water chestnuts, cabbage, celery, peas, and carrots are tender-crisp.

8. Toss in the meat and pre-cooked pasta for approximately 2 minutes.

9. Combine the cornstarch and water in a mixing bowl and pour it over the pasta.

10. Cook, stirring constantly, until the sauce thickens, then remove from the heat.

11. If preferred, garnish with chopped green onion.

Fried rice

Serves 2-4 people.

Time to Prepare: 15 minutes

Time to cook: 10 minutes

Ingredients

2 tablespoons vegetable oil

1 medium onion, chopped

4 cloves garlic, minced
61

1 teaspoon ginger, minced

⅓ cup boneless chicken, diced

⅓ cup Chinese sausage or ham, chopped

Salt and pepper

½ cup frozen peas

½ cup carrot, cut into small cubes

Water, if needed

1 tablespoon sesame oil

2 tablespoons soy sauce

½ teaspoon sugar (optional)

¼ cup green onions, thinly sliced

2 cups cooked day-old rice

1 egg, fried (optional)

Garlic chili sauce

Directions

1. In a wok, heat the vegetable oil over medium-high heat.

2. Combine the onion, garlic, and ginger in a mixing bowl. Stir for 30 seconds to 1 minute, or until the mixture is aromatic.

3. Cook until the chicken is no longer pink, then add the Chinese sausage or ham and season with salt and pepper.

4. Cook until the carrot is soft. If the extra fluid is required to cook the carrots, add 1 tablespoon at a time.

5. If using, add the sesame oil, soy sauce, and sugar.

6. Stir in the rice well. With a spatula, scrape the bottom of the pan and pull the rice upwards to thoroughly combine.

7. Stir in the frozen peas.

8. Cook for 10 minutes, stirring often.

9. Gently fold in the green onion. Seasonings may be used to enhance the taste if desired.

10. Arrange on a serving plate with a fried egg (optional) and garlic chili sauce on the side.

Yang Chow Fried Rice

servings: 4 people

Time to Prepare: 30 minutes

Time to cook: 10 minutes

Ingredients

2 large eggs, scrambled (cooked)

2-3 tablespoons vegetable or peanut oil

1 medium onion, minced

½ cup ham, cut into cubes

½ cup Chinese roast pork

5 cups cooked or day-old rice, lumps broken

¾ cup frozen peas, thawed

4 ounces fresh shrimp, shelled and deveined

1 ½ teaspoons salt

¼ teaspoon sugar

1 teaspoon rice wine

2 green onions, finely chopped

2 cups lettuce, finely chopped

⅛ teaspoon freshly ground white pepper

Directions

1. Cut the scrambled eggs into tiny pieces and leave them aside.

2. Bring some water to a boil in a saucepan to blanch the shrimp. Immerse the shrimp for a few seconds, or until the color changes to orange.

Take them out of the saucepan, drain, and put them aside.

3. Melt the butter in a wok over high heat. Stir in the onion and the oil.

Cook until the onion is transparent.

4. Cook for 30 seconds to heat through the ham and pork.

5. Stir in the rice for 2 minutes to cook it thoroughly. Remove any leftover lumps with the spatula, spraying water over any obstinate ones to soften them.

6. Cook, stirring regularly, for 2 minutes longer after adding the shrimp and peas.

7. Add the salt and sugar, and then dribble the wine along the rim of the wok.

8. Continue to mix, scraping the bottom of the pan with a spatula and raising the price higher. If necessary, moisten with water or add a bit of extra oil.

9. Combine the scrambled eggs, green onion, lettuce, and pepper in a mixing bowl and toss until the lettuce has wilted.

RECIPES FOR PORK

Pork Cooked Twice

Serves: 4

Time to Prepare: 10 minutes

Time to cook: 35 minutes

Ingredients:

2 quarts water

1 pound slab of pork belly

2 slices ginger

2 tablespoons oil, divided

1 ½ tablespoons spicy broad bean paste

2 cloves garlic, sliced

67

2 long hot green peppers, seeds removed and cut into 1 ½-inch

pieces

1 medium leek, split lengthwise, washed thoroughly, and cut in 2-

inch pieces

1 tablespoon rice wine

1 teaspoon soy sauce

¼ teaspoon sugar

Directions

1. Bring 2 quarts of water to a boil in a large saucepan.

2. Place the pork belly slab and ginger in a pot of boiling water.

Bring to a boil once more.

3. Reduce the heat to a low setting and continue to cook for 30 minutes, or until the pork is soft and cooked through.

4. Remove the pork from the saucepan and rinse it under cold running water for 1 minute before placing it on a cooling rack to drain and set aside.

5. Gather all of the other ingredients before proceeding to the following step; otherwise, the pork will dry out.

6. Cut the pork into 18-inch thick pieces.

7. Melt the butter in a wok over high heat. 1 tablespoon of oil should be added and swirled around.

8. Sear the pork pieces for 1 to 2 minutes, or until gently caramelized. Turn the heat down to medium-low.

9. Take the pork out of the skillet and put it aside.

10. In a separate pan, heat the remaining oil and add the bean paste. Allow it to cook for approximately 30 seconds, or until it is aromatic. Take care not to burn the bean paste, which should be red in color.

11. Stir in the garlic. Increase the heat to high and return the pork to the wok.

12. Combine the peppers, leeks, wine, and sugar in a mixing bowl. When the leeks have wilted, the meal is ready.

Moo Shu Pork

Serves 4 people.

Time to prepare: 45 minutes

Time to cook: 15 minutes

Ingredients:

For pancakes

2 cups flour, unshifted

¾ cup water

Sesame oil

For filling:

3 eggs, scrambled (cooked)

3 tablespoons canola oil

1 pound pork, julienned

1 tablespoon garlic, minced

1 tablespoon ginger, minced

2 cups white cabbage, shredded

¾ cup bamboo shoots, rinsed well, drained and julienned

½ red bell pepper, trimmed and finely julienned

¾ cup wood ear mushrooms, soaked in water overnight

(refrigerated) to rehydrate, sliced

1 cup shiitake mushrooms, sliced

10 dried lily buds, soaked in water overnight (refrigerated) to

rehydrate

1 cup hoisin sauce

1-2 tablespoons rice wine

1 bunch green onion or scallions, leaves slit several times to make a

scallion brush

Salt and pepper

Directions

<u>For the pancakes</u>

1. Bring water to a boil.

2. Make a well in the middle of the flour in a basin.

3. Stir in the heated water. To make a kneadable dough, gradually add additional flour.

4. Knead the dough for 5 minutes on a floured surface, then cover and set aside for 30 minutes.

5. Knead it for 5 minutes more, then shape it into a 12-inch cylinder.

6. Cut the cylinder into 16 pieces and roll each into a smooth ball.

7. Apply sesame oil to your hands and flatten a ball of dough.

8. Roll it into a smooth disc and brush it with sesame oil on top.

Make a second disc of comparable size and set it on top of the first. Roll them into a 6- to 7-inch-wide double disc.

Repeat with the remaining dough balls.

9. Heat a pan over medium heat until water drops in it bounces about in little balls. Apply a thin layer of sesame oil. Cook the double pancakes for 30 seconds on each side, no browning is required.

Take them out of the pan and smack them against a hard surface to separate the two discs. Peel the two discs apart and set them on a piece of foil. Rep this method for the remaining discs.

To steam the pancakes, make a package by wrapping foil around the discs. Steam the foil package for 20-30 minutes in a steamer or double boiler.

11. Serve immediately.

Heat a wok over high heat for filling 12. Cook the pork for 1 minute in the oil before removing it from the pan. Set it on a plate lined with paper towels to drain.

13. Stir-fry the garlic, ginger, and ear mushrooms in the pan for 2-3 minutes. Season with salt and pepper to taste.

14. Combine the cabbage, bamboo shoots, red bell pepper, remaining mushrooms, and lily buds in a mixing bowl. Cook for another 3-4 minutes.

15. Combine half of the hoisin sauce and the wine in a mixing bowl. Adjust the seasoning with salt and pepper to taste.

16. Place a heated pancake or tortilla on a clean surface and pour some hoisin sauce on it using the scallion brush.

17. Place a tablespoon of the pork mixture on top. Roll it up with a bit of extra hoisin sauce on top.

18. Continue until all of the pancakes have been utilized, then serve hot.

Chops de pork de Shanghai

Servings : 4

Preparation Time: 5 minutes, plus 2 hours marinating

Time to cook: 10 minutes.

74

Ingredients

4 pork chops

For marinade

½ cup light brown sugar

½ cup soy sauce

¼ cup ketchup

3 green onions, thinly sliced

1 teaspoon fresh ginger, peeled and grated

1 teaspoon garlic, minced

Directions:

1. Combine the marinade ingredients. Put it in a shallow container with a cover or a resealable plastic bag.

2. Toss the pork chops in the marinade to coat. Refrigerate the container for at least 2 hours after scaling it.

3. Grill the pork chops for 8-10 minutes on each side over medium-high heat on a prepared grill.

Ribs Roasted in China

Serves: 6 people

Time to prepare: 20 minutes

1 hour and 30 minutes of cooking time

Ingredients

1 large rack of ribs

For marinade

5 cloves garlic, minced

1 tablespoon pineapple, minced

76

2 tablespoons pineapple juice

1 tablespoon freshly-squeezed lime juice

1 tablespoon salt

⅓ cup sugar

1 tablespoon honey

2 tablespoons peanut oil

2 tablespoons hoisin sauce

1 teaspoon ground bean sauce

1 tablespoon tomato paste

1 tablespoon water

⅓ cup ketchup

½ tablespoon 5-spice powder

1 teaspoon fresh ground pepper

½ tablespoon paprika

1-star anise, ground

Directions

1. In a mixing dish, combine all of the marinade ingredients.

2. Brush the ribs with the marinade. Marinate them in the refrigerator overnight, covered with foil or plastic wrap.

3. Preheat the oven to 325°F and prepare a roasting pan with foil. Fill the container with water to a depth of 12 inches.

4. Place the roasting rack in the pan and place the ribs on it, rib-side up.

5. Bake for 30 minutes, then flip the ribs over and bake for another 60 minutes. If necessary, replenish the water in the pan to keep the ribs from drying out.

6. If preferred, broil for a few minutes to get a deeper color.

Sweet and Sour Pork

Serves: 2

Prep Time: 10 minutes + 30 minutes marinating

Time to cook: 20 minutes.

Ingredients

8 ounces boneless pork shoulder, cut into bite-size pieces

Sauce

⅛ teaspoon salt

1 tablespoon sugar

2 teaspoons rice wine

2 teaspoons rice vinegar

1 tablespoon soy sauce

2 tablespoon plum sauce

¾ teaspoon cornstarch

¼ cup water

For marinade

2 teaspoons rice wine

½ teaspoon oyster sauce

½ teaspoon regular soy sauce

Other ingredients

1 egg

Cooking oil for deep-frying plus 2 teaspoons for sautéing

1 teaspoon plus about ⅓ cup cornstarch

1 onion, sliced

1 thumb ginger, peeled and minced

½ cup pineapple cubes

2 bell peppers, cut into 1-inch pieces

1 small ripe tomato, cut into wedges

1 green onion, thinly sliced

Cooked rice, for serving

Directions

1. In a mixing dish, combine all of the sauce ingredients and put them aside.

2. Combine the marinade ingredients in a mixing bowl. Stir in the pork and set aside for 30 minutes to marinate.

80

3. In a medium-sized mixing bowl, whisk the egg, and place the cornstarch on a plate.

4. After marinating, dip the pork in the beaten egg, followed by the cornstarch. Allow the meat to sit for 3 minutes after thoroughly coating it.

5. Heat a wok and pour oil to a depth of approximately 34 inches. Preheat the oil to 350°F.

6. Fry the pork in batches for 2-3 minutes, then drain on a paper towel-lined plate. Heat the wok to 375°F once all of the pieces have been pre-fried. Place all of the meat in the fryer and cook until it is brown and crisp.

7. Preheat a clean wok on high heat. 2 tablespoons oil, as well as the onion, ginger, and pineapple Cook for 2 minutes, or until the pineapple starts to caramelize. Cook, stirring constantly until the bell pepper is tender-crisp.

8. Combine the sauce and tomato in a mixing bowl. Cook until it starts to thicken and boil.

9. Add the pork and toss to coat thoroughly. Take the wok off the heat.

10. Garnish with green onions and serve over rice.

Snow Peas with Pork

Serves : 4-6 people

Preparation Time required: 10 minutes, plus 30-40 minutes for marinating.

Time to cook: 15 minutes

Ingredients

1 pound pork tenderloin, cubed

82

2 tablespoons peanut (or other preferred oil)

1 teaspoon cornstarch

1 pound of snow peas, cleaned and trimmed

1 clove of garlic, crushed and minced

2 teaspoons fresh ginger, minced or grated

½ cup water chestnuts

4-5 green onions, finely sliced, green parts only

1 ½ tablespoons hoisin sauce

For marinade:

2 tablespoons soy sauce

1 teaspoon rice wine

1 ½ teaspoon sesame oil

2 teaspoons sugar

4-5 green onions, finely sliced, white parts only

1 clove of garlic, crushed and minced

2 teaspoons fresh ginger, minced or grated

1 teaspoon cornstarch

Salt and pepper

Rice for serving

Directions

1. Make the marinade for the pork by combining all of the ingredients in a medium or large mixing basin. Whisk until smooth.

Toss the diced pork in the basin lightly. Refrigerate for 30-60 minutes, covered.

2. Heat a wok over medium-high heat. Add just enough peanut oil to cover the bottom, leaving some at the bottom.

3. While the oil is heating, prepare a smooth, thin paste with one teaspoon of cornstarch and adequate water. Save this for later use.

4. Toss in the snow peas, garlic, ginger, and water chestnuts. Cook, stirring gently for about 1-2 minutes, or until the snow peas begin to become a brighter green. Season with salt and pepper to taste, then remove from the pan and put aside.

5. Re-heat the wok and add extra peanut oil if necessary. Sauté the pork, including the marinade, until golden brown, about 2-3 minutes.

6. Once the pork is cooked, add the snow pea mixture back to the pan.

Combine the green onions, hoisin sauce, and cornstarch mixture in a mixing bowl. Cook for 3 minutes, or until the sauce starts to thicken, tossing the ingredients gently to coat.

7. Serve right away with rice.

BEEF RECIPES

Snow Peas with Pork

Serves: 4-6 people

Preparation Time required: 10 minutes, plus 30-40 minutes for marinating.

Time to cook: 15 minutes

85

Ingredients

12 ounces beef tenderloin, thinly sliced

¼ cup oil for frying

For marinade

¼ teaspoon salt

¼ teaspoon sugar

½ teaspoon white pepper

1 tablespoon soy sauce

1 teaspoon vinegar

For sauce

1 ½ teaspoons cornstarch

1 tablespoon water

2 tablespoons rice vinegar

2 tablespoons granulated sugar

1 tablespoon light soy sauce

1 tablespoon dark soy sauce

2 teaspoons Chinese rice wine or dry sherry

½ teaspoon chili sauce

¼ teaspoon sesame oil

4 cloves garlic, chopped

1 medium white onion, chopped

½ cup green onions, sliced

10 water chestnuts, sliced

Chicken stock or water, as needed

Directions:

1. Make the marinade for the pork by combining all of the ingredients in a medium or large mixing basin. Whisk until smooth.

Toss the diced pork in the basin lightly. Refrigerate for 30-60 minutes, covered.

2. Heat a wok over medium-high heat. Add just enough peanut oil to cover the bottom, leaving some at the bottom.

3. While the oil is heating, prepare a smooth, thin paste with one teaspoon of cornstarch and adequate water. Save this for later use.

4. Toss in the snow peas, garlic, ginger, and water chestnuts. Cook, stirring gently for about 1-2 minutes, or until the snow peas begin to become a brighter green. Season with salt and pepper to taste, then remove from the pan and put aside.

5. Re-heat the wok and add extra peanut oil if necessary. Sauté the pork, including the marinade, until golden brown, about 2-3 minutes.

6. Once the pork is cooked, add the snow pea mixture back to the pan.

Combine the green onions, hoisin sauce, and cornstarch mixture in a mixing bowl. Cook for 3 minutes, or until the sauce starts to thicken, tossing the ingredients gently to coat.

7. Serve right away with rice.

Recipe for Szechuan Beef

Preparation Time: 20 minutes Servings: 2

Time to cook: 5 minutes

Ingredients

8 ounces beef tenderloin, cut into strips

Marinade

1 teaspoon cornstarch

½ teaspoon rice wine

1 teaspoon dark soy sauce

Sauce

½ tablespoon oyster sauce

½ tablespoon chili garlic sauce

1 ½ teaspoons soy sauce

2 teaspoons sugar

2 tablespoons water

½ teaspoon chili oil

½ teaspoon sesame oil

Other ingredients

89

2 tablespoons oil, divided

2 cloves garlic, minced

¼ small green bell pepper, julienned

¼ small red bell pepper, julienned

1 small carrot, julienned

½ teaspoon chili oil or according to taste

2 stalks of green onion, cut into strips

Directions

1. Combine the marinade ingredients. Marinate the meat for 15-30 minutes, stirring occasionally.

2. Combine the sauce ingredients in a mixing basin and put them aside.

3. Melt the butter in a wok over high heat. Sear the meat in 1 tablespoon of oil until it is partially browned. Place it on a platter lined with paper.

4. Remove any burnt parts from the wok and pour in the remaining oil.

5. Stir in the garlic until it is aromatic.

6. Add the peppers and carrots and mix well. Cook for 30 seconds before returning the steak to the wok.

7. Pour in the sauce mixture and well mix it up.

8. Combine the green onion and chili oil in a mixing bowl. Stir for 30 seconds, or until the sauce reaches the desired consistency.

9. Distribute.

Recipe for Szechuan Beef

Servings: 2

Preparation Time: 20 minutes

Time to cook: 5 minutes

Ingredients

91

For marinade

1 tablespoon rice wine

2 teaspoons oyster sauce

1 teaspoon cornstarch

White pepper

Slurry/Thickener

¾ cups chicken stock

1 teaspoon cornstarch

2-3 tablespoons peanut oil, as needed

½ pound skirt steak, cut into strips

2 cloves garlic, minced

½ stalk celery, diced

½ onion, minced

½ carrot, shredded

3 button mushrooms, sliced

½ cup broccoli florets

10 snow peas, trimmed,

1 ½ teaspoon sesame oil

Rice or noodles for serving

Directions

1. Combine the marinade ingredients. Marinate the meat for 15-30 minutes, stirring occasionally.

2. Combine the sauce ingredients in a mixing basin and put them aside.

3. Melt the butter in a wok over high heat. Sear the meat in 1 tablespoon of oil until it is partially browned. Place it on a platter lined with paper.

4. Remove any burnt parts from the wok and pour in the remaining oil.

5. Stir in the garlic until it is aromatic.

6. Add the peppers and carrots and mix well. Cook for 30 seconds before returning the steak to the wok.

7. Pour in the sauce mixture and well mix it up.

8. Combine the green onion and chili oil in a mixing bowl. Stir for 30 seconds, or until the sauce reaches the desired consistency.

9. Distribute.

Oyster Sauced Beef

Serve : 2-4 people

Time to prepare: 5 minutes + 30 minutes marinating

Time to cook: 12 minutes

Ingredients

1 pound beef tenderloin, thinly sliced

1 tablespoon ginger, minced

1 tablespoon garlic, minced

2 teaspoons chili, minced (optional)

94

2 cups fresh spinach, cleaned

3 tablespoons cooking oil

For marinade

2 tablespoons oyster sauce

1 tablespoon soy sauce

1 teaspoon salt

½ teaspoon ground black pepper

Directions

1. Combine the marinade ingredients and marinate the meat for 30 minutes.

2. Heat the frying oil in a wok over high heat.

3. Cook until the ginger, garlic, and chile are aromatic.

4. Stir in the spinach until it is wilted.

5. Remove the veggies from the pan, leaving as much oil as possible behind, and place them on a serving dish.

6. Fry the marinated meat in the remaining oil in the pan until it is cooked and browned.

7. Place the cooked meat on top of the spinach mixture.

Beef with Ginger

2-3 servings

Time to Prepare: 30 minutes

Time to cook: 15 minutes

Ingredients

1 pound flank steak, sliced thinly

For marinade

2 tablespoons dark soy sauce

1 tablespoon rice wine

1 teaspoon sugar

1 tablespoon minced

For sauce

1 tablespoon rice wine

1 tablespoon light soy sauce

2 tablespoons rice vinegar

2 tablespoons sugar

2 tablespoons water

Hot chili oil or crushed red pepper flakes, to taste

For batter

¼ cup flour

¼ cup cornstarch

1 tablespoon vegetable oil

1 tablespoon hot chili oil (optional)

⅓ cup water, or as needed

Other ingredients

4 to 5 cups oil for deep frying

2 tablespoons oil for stir-frying, or as needed

3 red chili peppers, seeds left in, chopped

2 cloves garlic, minced

1 tablespoon fresh ginger, minced

1 small carrot, julienned

1 stalk celery, cut into thin strips

1 red bell pepper, julienned

1 teaspoon sesame oil

Directions

1. Combine the marinade ingredients and marinate the meat for 30 minutes.

2. In a small dish, combine the sauce ingredients and put them aside.

3. Gather all of the ingredients.

4. Begin by combining the flour and cornstarch in a mixing bowl.

Create a well in the middle and pour in the oil and chili oil (optional).

Mix while gently adding the water. Use just enough water to get the desired consistency. When the batter softly drips off the back of a wooden spoon, it's ready.

5. Dredge the marinated meat in the batter.

6. Heat the wok to high heat. Heat the frying oil to 350°F in a saucepan.

7. Fry the steak in a deep fryer until golden brown. Remove it from the oil and place it on a dish lined with paper towels.

8. Preheat the oil to 400°F.

9. Fry the steak until crispy again, then remove it from the pan.

10. Heat the oil for stir-frying in a clean wok over high heat.

Stir in the chiles, garlic, and ginger. Sauté until the chilies begin to blister and become aromatic.

11. Cook for approximately 1 minute after adding the carrot.

12 Stir in the celery and bell pepper. Stir-fry for about 30 seconds.

13. Push the veggies to the edges of the wok and add the sauce mixture.

14. Bring it to a boil (watch carefully so the veggies don't burn) and then add the fried meat.

15. Combine all ingredients in a mixing bowl and heat thoroughly.

16. Remove from the fire, add the sesame oil, and serve.

Steak with Chinese Peppers

Serves: 4-6 people

Time to prepare: 10 minutes + 2-4 hours marinating time

Time to cook: 15 minutes

Ingredients

1 pound flank steak, sliced very thinly against the grain

4 tablespoons soy sauce

½ cup sherry

100

1 tablespoon ginger, minced

5 cloves garlic, minced

1 tablespoon coarsely ground black pepper

½-1 teaspoon crushed dried chilies, more if you want it very spicy

1 tablespoon cornstarch

1 large yellow onion, sliced

2 green bell peppers, sliced

½ teaspoon salt

4 tablespoons peanut oil

Rice for serving

Directions

1. Whisk together the soy sauce, sherry, ginger, garlic, black pepper, chiles, and cornstarch in a large mixing basin. Whisk until all of the ingredients are combined. Refrigerate for 2-4 hours after adding the meat and tossing till coated.

2. Heat three tablespoons of Sepeanut oil in a hot skillet or wok over high heat. Brown the steak rapidly, stirring for no more than 20 seconds, being careful not to crowd the pan. Remove the steak from the pan and put it aside.

3. If necessary, add extra oil and stir-fry the bell peppers and onion with salt. Cook for 3-4 minutes, or until the peppers are soft.

4. Return the steak to the pan, along with the remaining marinade.

Reduce the heat to low and continue to cook until the sauce thickens.

5. Serve with rice of your choice.

Beef with Broccoli

Serves: 4

Preparation time: 10 minutes

Time to cook: 20 minutes

Ingredients

1 pound beef, sliced into thin strips

2-3 tablespoons cooking or peanut oil

3 cloves garlic, minced

1 cup beef broth

½ cup soy sauce

⅓ cup brown sugar

2 tablespoons cornstarch

4 tablespoons water

2 cups frozen broccoli florets

1 tablespoon sesame oil

White rice, cooked

Directions

1. In a wok, heat the oil over high heat. Fry the beef in 2 teaspoons of oil until it is browned. It should be drained on paper towels.

2. Heat the remaining oil in the wok (approximately 1 tablespoon extra if necessary) and sauté the garlic until fragrant.

103

3. Combine the broth, soy sauce, and sugar in a mixing bowl. Bring the water to a boil.

4. Add the fried meat back to the sauce. Allow it to simmer, covered, for approximately 10 minutes, or until the vegetables are soft.

5. Remove approximately 14 cup of the sauce from the pan and transfer to a small bowl.

6. Make a slurry of cornstarch and water and mix it into the wok.

7. Add the broccoli and simmer for approximately 30 seconds, stirring constantly, to thicken the sauce and heat through.

8. Drizzle with sesame oil and serve immediately over rice.

Beef Kung Pao

4-6 people

1 hour and 10 minutes to prepare

Time to cook: 15 minutes

Ingredients

1 pound flank or flat iron steak

1 tablespoon soy sauce

2 tablespoons sesame oil

1 tablespoon dry sherry

6 cloves garlic, minced (divided)

105

2 tablespoons peanut oil

4 dried red chilies, split

½ tablespoon grated ginger

1 teaspoon Szechwan peppercorns, crushed

2 green onions, sliced white and green parts in ½ -inch pieces

1 red bell pepper, trimmed and cubed

For sauce:

2 tablespoons soy sauce

3 tablespoons of dry sherry

2 tablespoons balsamic vinegar

1 teaspoon sugar

1 cup vegetable broth

1 tablespoon cornstarch

½ cup roasted peanuts

Rice for serving

Directions

1. Combine the soy sauce, sesame oil, dry sherry, and 2 minced garlic cloves in a large mixing bowl. Turn the steak to cover it with the sauce.

Marinate for a minimum of one hour.

2. In a mixing dish, combine all of the sauce ingredients. Set away from the whisk.

3. Heat the peanut oil in a big pan or wok over high heat. After 30 seconds, add the red chilies, ginger, and Szechuan peppercorns to the oil. 1 minute of stirring

4. Stir in the rest of the garlic, green onions, and bell pepper. Stir fry for 3 minutes before adding the beef. Cook for another 2-3 minutes.

5. Combine the sauce in a mixing bowl and add it to the pan. Simmer for 3-4 minutes, or until the sauce thickens.

6. Stir in the peanuts.

7. Plate with rice.

Beef with Sesame Seeds

4 servings

Time to Prepare: 40 minutes

Time to cook: 15 minutes

Ingredients

2 tablespoons soy sauce

2 tablespoons dry sherry

1 tablespoon sugar

2 teaspoons rice vinegar

½ teaspoon red pepper flakes

½ teaspoon cornstarch

1 pound boneless sirloin steak, thinly sliced in strips against the

grain

1 tablespoon sesame seeds

1 tablespoon peanut oil

2 teaspoons sesame oil

2-3 cloves garlic, minced

Rice for serving

Directions

1. In a small bowl, whisk together the soy sauce, dry sherry, sugar, rice vinegar, red pepper flakes, and cornstarch until well combined. Combine the mixture and the sirloin steak strips in a resealable bag. Turn to coat, and place in the refrigerator for at least 30 minutes to marinate. Remove the steak to a platter and set aside the leftover marinating sauce.

2. Toast the sesame seeds in a small dry pan over medium heat until fragrant, approximately 1 minute.

3. Heat a large skillet or wok over medium-high heat. Heat for another 30 seconds after adding both oils. Add the

garlic and steak slices once the oil is heated. For around 3 minutes, stir fry.

4. Add the remaining marinade sauce and mix well. Cook for 1-2 minutes over medium heat, stirring to coat.

5. Once the sauce has thickened, stir in the toasted sesame seeds.

Serve with rice.

Beef in Orange

Serves: 4-6 people

Time to Prepare: 15 minutes

Time to cook: 10 minutes

Ingredients

½ pound flat iron steak, sliced thinly

1 egg white

1 large orange, zested and juiced

3 tablespoons soy sauce

3 tablespoons sherry

3 tablespoons rice wine vinegar

2 teaspoons chili garlic sauce

2 teaspoons sesame oil

5 green onions, sliced, greens reserved for garnish

1 tablespoon sugar

1 teaspoon baking soda

¾ cup cornstarch, divided

Peanut oil for frying (or other preferred oil)

Rice for serving

Directions

1. Apply an even application of baking soda to the steak. Refrigerate in a basin until ready to use.

2. Combine orange juice, sherry, soy sauce, and rice wine vinegar in a small bowl. Whisk in 2 teaspoons of cornstarch until the sauce is clump-free, then add the sugar to dissolve.

3. In a small dish, place the egg white. Remove the meat from the refrigerator and mix with the egg white to coat evenly. Toss the meat with the cornstarch to coat it. Continue to add cornstarch until the meat has a thick, uniform layer.

4. Heat the oil in a wok over high heat. The oil level in the pan should be high enough to thoroughly immerse the pieces of meat.

5. Once the oil is heated, use a slotted spatula to carefully drop the meat into the pan. Fry for 3-5 minutes, or until the coating is crisp and golden brown. Remove the meat from the pan and lay it on a platter lined with paper towels to collect any leftover oil. When cooking the meat, do not overcrowd the pan.

Meat may need to be cooked in multiple smaller batches depending on the size of the wok.

6. Remove the wok from the heat and set aside for a few minutes to let the oil cool.

Keep enough oil to coat the pan and discard the rest. Stir in the green onions and chile paste. Toss for 1-2 minutes, or until aromatic. Add the prepared sauce mixture, orange zest, and sesame oil to the pan. Bring mixture to a boil and simmer for 2 minutes, or until thickened.

Return the beef to the pan and stir to coat. Warm over low to medium heat for approximately 1-2 minutes, or until well heated.

113

8. Serve with rice right away.

9. If preferred, garnish with green onions.

RECIPES FOR CHICKEN AND DUCK

The Empress Chicken

servings : 4

Time to prepare: 5 minutes + 30 minutes marinating

Time to cook: 15 minutes

Ingredients

For marinade

2 tablespoons cornstarch

1 tablespoon soy sauce

For sauce

1 tablespoon rice wine

2 tablespoons soy sauce

1 tablespoon sugar

1 teaspoon salt

1 teaspoon cornstarch

1 teaspoon sesame oil

1 pound boneless chicken, chopped into 1-inch pieces

1 cup cooking oil

10 dried hot red peppers or according to taste

1 teaspoon Sichuan peppercorns (Chinese coriander)

1 teaspoon ginger, minced

4 cups rice for serving

Directions

1. In a mixing basin, combine the chicken, cornstarch, and soy sauce. Allow it to marinate for 30 minutes.

2. Combine the sauce ingredients and put them aside.

3. Heat a wok over high heat after the chicken is done. Fry the marinated chicken in the oil until it is browned. Transfer it to a cooling rack or paper towels using a slotted spoon or spider strainer.

4. Pour off any extra oil from the pan, if there are more than 2 tablespoons.

5. For approximately 30 seconds, sauté the dried peppers and Sichuan peppercorns.

6. Add the pre-fried chicken back to the wok. Stir in the ginger and cook for 1 minute.

7. Add the sauce and heat until it thickens.

8. Serve immediately with rice.

Recipe for Moo Goo Gai Pan

Servings :3

Time to prepare: 30 minutes

Time to cook: 15 minutes

Ingredients

10 ounces chicken breast fillet, cut into thin slices

⅓ cup vegetable or peanut oil

For marinade

1 egg white, lightly beaten

⅛ teaspoon ground white pepper

½ teaspoon salt

117

For sauce

¼ cup chicken broth

1 tablespoon light soy sauce

¼ teaspoon sesame oil

½ tablespoon sugar

3 dashes of ground white pepper

1 tablespoon rice wine

1 teaspoon cornstarch

Other ingredients

3 cloves garlic, peeled and minced

1 baby carrot, peeled and sliced thinly

½ of snow peas, trimmed

½ cup button mushrooms, sliced

½ cup straw mushrooms, sliced

½ teaspoon sugar

Salt to taste

Cooked rice, for serving

Directions

1. Combine the marinade ingredients. Combine thoroughly.

2. Marinate the chicken pieces for approximately 10 minutes, ensuring sure they're all well-coated, and then drain off any excess marinade.

3. Melt the butter in a wok over high heat. Heat the oil until it reaches nearly blazing temperature.

4. Cook the chicken in a skillet until it is halfway done (about 45 seconds).

5. Remove the chicken from the pan with a slotted spoon and drain it on paper towels. Set it aside for now.

6. Pour 2 tablespoons of oil into a clean wok.

7. Stir-fry the garlic until it begins to brown.

8. Stir in the carrot and snow peas for 2 minutes.

9. Stir in the mushrooms for another 2 minutes.

10. Combine the chicken and sauce ingredients in a mixing bowl. Stir everything together well.

11. Simmer, covered, until the chicken is cooked through and the sauce has thickened.

12. Season with salt and sugar to taste, and serve over rice.

Lemon Chicken

serves : 12 people

Time to prepare: 5 minutes + 15 minutes marinating

Time to cook: 30 minutes

Ingredients

3 pounds chicken breast fillets, halved

For marinade

1 tablespoon rice wine

1 tablespoon soy sauce

½ teaspoon salt

For batter

2 large eggs, beaten

¼ cup cornstarch

½ teaspoon baking powder

Other ingredients

2 cups vegetable oil, for frying

2 tablespoons vegetable oil

1 lemon, sliced

1 cup chicken broth

⅓ cup sugar

1 tablespoon cornstarch

1 tablespoon lemon juice

1 teaspoon salt

Directions

1. Combine the marinade ingredients and marinate the chicken for 15 minutes.

2. When the chicken is done, combine the batter ingredients. Dip the chicken in the batter, thoroughly coating each piece.

3. Heat the oil for frying in a wok over high heat. Reduce the heat to medium-high and continue to cook the chicken until it is brown in color. Remove it and pat it dry with paper towels.

4. Arrange the chicken in bite-size pieces on a serving platter.

5. Heat 2 tablespoons oil in a nonstick frying pan over medium heat and stir-fry the lemon slices.

6. In a separate basin, quickly combine the remaining chicken broth, sugar, cornstarch, lemon juice, and salt, and pour it over the lemon segments.

7. Cook for another 3 minutes, or until the sauce has thickened and become transparent.

8. Drizzle the sauce over the chicken and serve immediately.

Pancakes and Crispy Duck

servings:4

Time to prepare: 20 minutes + overnight salting

Time to cook: 1 1/2 to 2 hours

Ingredients

4 whole duck legs

For overnight salting

1 teaspoon 5-spice powder

1 teaspoon Sichuan peppercorns, crushed

1 teaspoon salt

For baking

1 teaspoon honey

¾ cup chicken stock

For pancakes

2 cups flour, unsifted

¾ cup water

123

Sesame oil

For serving

Spring onions, julienned

Cucumber sticks

Hoisin sauce

Directions

1. Using a fork or knife, prick the duck legs all over. The salting components should be rubbed into the duck legs. Allow them to sit overnight or for a few hours, covered and refrigerated.

2. Preheat the oven to 400 degrees Fahrenheit and blot the duck legs dry with paper towels.

3. Place the duck legs in a nonstick frying pan, skin side down.

4. Cook, without rotating, over high heat until the skin starts to crisp and brown (about 5 minutes). Turn them over and brown the other side.

5. Place the browned duck legs in a baking dish or oven-safe dish.

6. Drizzle with honey and add the chicken stock.

7. Bake for 20 minutes, then decrease to 275°F and bake for 1 hour. At this time, the duck flesh should be falling off the bone.

8. Prepare the pancake batter while the duck legs are baking. (See the list below.)

9. When the duck legs are done, take them from the oven and set them aside to cool for a few minutes.

10. Using two forks, shred the duck flesh, sprinkle with spring onion, and serve with hot pancakes, cucumber, and hoisin sauce.

Making Pancakes

1. Bring water to a boil.

2. Make a well in the middle of the flour in a basin.

3. Stir in the heated water. To make a kneadable dough, gradually add additional flour.

4. Knead the dough for 5 minutes on a floured surface, then cover and set aside for 30 minutes.

5. Knead it for 5 minutes more, then shape it into a 12-inch cylinder.

6. Cut the cylinder into 16 pieces and roll each into a smooth ball.

7. Apply sesame oil to your hands and flatten a ball of dough.

125

8. Roll it into a smooth disc and brush it with sesame oil on top.

Make a second disc of comparable size and set it on top of the first. Roll them into a 6- to 7-inch-wide double disc.

Repeat with the remaining dough balls.

9. Heat a pan over medium heat until water drops in it bounce about in little balls. Apply a thin layer of sesame oil. Cook the double pancakes for 30 seconds on each side, no browning is required.

Take them out of the pan and smack them against a hard surface to separate the two discs. Peel the two discs apart and set them on a piece of foil. Rep this method for the remaining discs.

To steam the pancakes, make a package by wrapping foil around the discs. Steam the foil package for 20-30 minutes in a steamer or double boiler.

Chicken with Sesame Sauce

Time to prepare: 10-15 minutes

Time to cook: 15 minutes

Ingredients

6 skinless chicken fillets, halved

2 tablespoons sesame seeds

For basting

2 tablespoons lemon juice

2 tablespoons soy sauce

¼ cup ketchup

1 tablespoon sesame oil

¼ teaspoon ground ginger

2 teaspoons brown sugar

Directions

1. Preheat a grill to medium-high heat and blot dry the chicken with paper towels.

2. Combine the basting ingredients.

3. Grill the chicken for 10-13 minutes, rotating regularly and brushing or basting with the mixture.

4. The chicken is done when the juices flow clear and there is no longer any hint of pink.

5. Before serving, remove the chicken from the grill and sprinkle it with sesame seeds.

Recipe for Kung Pao Chicken

3-4 servings

Time to Prepare: 15 minutes

Time to cook: 10 minutes

Ingredients

For marinade

2 teaspoons soy sauce

2 teaspoons Chinese rice wine

2 teaspoons cornstarch

1 teaspoon Sichuan peppercorns

For sauce

1 tablespoon Chinese black vinegar

1 tablespoon chicken stock

3 teaspoons sugar

2-3 teaspoons soy sauce

2 teaspoons cornstarch

1/2 teaspoon sesame oil

Other ingredients

1 pound skinless boneless chicken breasts, cut into 1/2 - inch cubes

1 tablespoon peanut or vegetable oil

8 dried red chilies, split lengthwise and seeds removed

1 teaspoon Sichuan peppercorns

4 cloves garlic, minced

1 tablespoon fresh ginger, minced

3 scallions, white parts thinly sliced, green parts set aside cut into 1-

inch strips

⅓ cup unsalted dry-roasted peanuts

130

Directions

1. Combine the marinade ingredients and marinate the chicken for 20 minutes.

2. Combine the sauce ingredients in a mixing basin and put them aside.

3. Heat a wok over high heat until it is almost smoking. Pour in the oil.

4. Remove from the fire and stir in the red peppers and Sichuan peppercorns. Cook for 1 minute, stirring constantly. Take care not to burn the chiles.

5. Replace the lid and return the heat to medium-high.

6. Stir-fry the marinated chicken until it is halfway done.

7. Add the garlic and ginger and simmer for another 2 minutes.

8. Add the sauce gradually, one spoonful at a time. Allow the flavors to permeate the chicken as it cooks.

9. Add the green onion and peanuts when the chicken is done.

Serve immediately

General Tso's Chicken

servings: 4 people

Preparation 1 hour and 15 minutes

Time to cook: 10 minutes

Ingredients

4 pieces of chicken fillet, cut into 1-inch pieces

For the marinade and sauce

½ cup hoisin sauce

¼ cup white vinegar

3 tablespoons soy sauce

3 tablespoons sugar

2 tablespoons cornstarch
132

1 ½ cups water

For sautéing

1 tablespoon vegetable oil

4 cloves garlic, minced

2 tablespoons grated fresh ginger

½ teaspoon red pepper flakes, crushed

For coating and deep-frying

3 egg whites

1 ½ cups cornstarch

½ cup all-purpose flour

½ teaspoon baking soda

4 cups vegetable oil

For garnish

2 green onions, chopped

Directions

1. In a mixing dish, combine the marinade ingredients. 13 cups of the marinade should be separated and chilled for 30 minutes before marinating the chicken. Set out the remainder for the sauce.

2. Heat the oil in a wok over high heat. Reduce the heat to medium-high and add the garlic, ginger, and pepper flakes to the pan.

Cook until fragrant.

3. Add the remaining sauce mixture (approximately 2 cups) and continue to simmer, stirring regularly, until thickened. Remove from the heat and cover with a lid. Maintain the temperature.

4. Whisk the egg whites until foamy in a mixing basin. In a separate dish, add the other coating ingredients and mix until the consistency is equivalent to a coarse meal.

5. Remove the marinated chicken from the dish and wipe it dry with paper towels.

Each piece should be dipped in the egg whites and then coated in the cornstarch mixture.

6. Fry the chicken at 350°F for 3 minutes, or until golden brown. Using paper towels, drain.

7. Bring the sauce back up to a simmer. Stir in the chicken to coat.

8. Distribute

Stir-Fry with Orange Chicken and Vegetables Serves: 4-6 people

Time to Prepare: 15 minutes

Time to cook: 10 minutes.

Stir-Fry with Orange Chicken and Vegetables

Serves: 4-6 people

Time to Prepare: 15 minutes

Time to cook: 10 minutes.

Ingredients

135

For sauce

½ cup orange juice

2 tablespoons soy sauce

2 tablespoons rice vinegar

1 tablespoon oyster sauce

1 tablespoon orange zest

2 cloves garlic

1 teaspoon ginger, peeled and minced

1 ½ teaspoon honey, or to taste

For stir-fry

1 pound chicken tenderloin, cut into bite-size pieces

Salt and pepper

3 tablespoons cornstarch

1 cup chopped broccoli, sliced

1 cup carrots, sliced

1 cup snow peas, trimmed

½ cup celery, sliced

½ cup mushrooms, sliced

2-3 tablespoons peanut or vegetable oil

½ cup medium yellow onion, chopped

Rice, for serving

Directions

1. In a blender, combine all of the sauce ingredients and puree for 10-15 seconds.

2. Place in a pot and bring to a boil. 5 minutes in the oven

3. Using paper towels, pat the chicken dry.

4. Combine the salt, pepper, and cornstarch in a mixing bowl, and coat the chicken with the mixture.

5. Boil enough water to cover the veggies in a pot or wok. Place the broccoli, carrots, snow peas, and mushrooms in a saucepan of boiling water and cook for 3-5 minutes.

Remove the veggies from the water and pat them dry using paper towels.

6. Melt the butter in a clean wok over medium-high heat. Fry the onions alongside the chicken for 3-5 minutes in the peanut oil.

7. Stir in the pre-boiled veggies for 2 minutes.

8. Gradually add the sauce while continually stirring and allowing a few seconds between additions. The sauce should thicken and coat the meat.

9. Serve immediately over rice.

Directions

1. In a blender, combine all of the sauce ingredients and puree for 10-15 seconds.

2. Place in a pot and bring to a boil. 5 minutes in the oven

3. Using paper towels, pat the chicken dry.

4. Combine the salt, pepper, and cornstarch in a mixing bowl, and coat the chicken with the mixture.

5. Boil enough water to cover the veggies in a pot or wok. Place the broccoli, carrots, snow peas, and mushrooms in a saucepan of boiling water and cook for 3-5 minutes.

Remove the veggies from the water and pat them dry using paper towels.

6. Melt the butter in a clean wok over medium-high heat. Fry the onions alongside the chicken for 3-5 minutes in the peanut oil.

7. Stir in the pre-boiled veggies for 2 minutes.

8. Gradually add the sauce while continually stirring and allowing a few seconds between additions. The sauce should thicken and coat the meat.

9. Serve immediately over rice.

Cashew Chicken is my favorite.

servings 4

Time to Prepare: 15 minutes

Time to cook: 15 minutes

Ingredients

1 cup raw unsalted cashews, coarsely chopped

1 tablespoon peanut (or other preferred oil)

1 ½ pound boneless, skinless chicken, cubed

5 cloves garlic, crushed and minced

½ small red bell pepper, cubed

5 scallions, diced, green parts reserved for garnish

½ teaspoon salt (optional)

139

½ teaspoon pepper (optional)

Small pinch of cayenne pepper, if desired

2 tablespoons rice vinegar

3 tablespoons hoisin sauce

1 teaspoon honey

1 ½ tablespoons soy sauce

¼ teaspoon sesame oil

3 tablespoons water

Cooked rice for serving

Directions

1. Preheat the oven to 350 degrees Fahrenheit.

2. Spread the cashews out on a baking sheet and toast for 5-7 minutes in the oven. Allow them to totally cool before using.

3. Heat 1 tablespoon peanut oil to extremely hot in a wok or big sauté pan. Combine the chicken, garlic, red bell pepper, white scallions, salt, pepper, and cayenne pepper in a mixing bowl.

4. Cook, turning gently until the chicken is golden brown, approximately 3-5 minutes. Cooking the chicken fully at this phase will result in an overdone final meal.

5. Depending on the size of your pan, you may need to cook the chicken in two batches to produce an even golden color on all pieces.

6. Whisk together the vinegar, hoisin sauce, honey, soy sauce, and sesame oil in a mixing bowl until thoroughly blended.

7. Add the sauce mixture to the pan and continue to cook until the flavors are mixed and the chicken is no longer pink and the juices run clear.

8. Take the skillet off the heat and add the roasted cashews. If desired, season with salt and pepper.

9. Serve immediately with cooked rice and, if preferred, garnish with scallion greens.

Sweet and sour chicken

servings: 4

141

Time to Prepare: 15 minutes

Time to cook: 25 minutes

Ingredients

1 pound boneless, skinless chicken, cubed

1 red bell pepper, seeded and cubed

1 green bell pepper, seeded and cubed

1 cup fresh pineapple, chunked

1 ½ cups vegetable oil for frying

Rice for serving

For sauce

1 ½ cups water

¾ cup sugar

½ cup rice wine vinegar

½ cup fresh pineapple juice

For slurry

¼ cup cornstarch

¼ cup water

For batter

2 ¼ cups flour

¼ cup cornstarch

2 tablespoons vegetable oil

1 egg, beaten

Salt and pepper (to taste)

1 ½ cups water

Directions

1. Start by making the sauce. 1 12 cup water, sugar, vinegar, and fresh pineapple juice in a medium saucepan

2. In a separate small dish, combine the cornstarch and water to produce the slurry. Whisk until thoroughly combined and free of clumps.

3. Bring the sauce to a boil in a saucepan, then remove from the heat. Slowly whisk in the cornstarch mixture until it is completely integrated and the liquid starts to thicken slightly.

Set aside the sauce.

4. To create the batter, whisk together the flour, cornstarch, oil, egg, and salt & pepper to taste in a separate basin. Whisk everything together until smooth.

143

5. Stir in up to 12 cups of water at a time until a thick batter forms. It should be thick enough to form a medium-to-thick coat on the chicken.

6. Toss the cubed chicken in the butter until evenly covered.

7. Heat the frying oil in a wok or big sauté pan over medium-high heat. A quick read thermometer should read 350oF.

8. Once the oil is heated, fry the chicken pieces in batches for 10-15 minutes, or until crispy and golden brown.

9. Remove the chicken from the oil and drain any excess.

Remove any remaining oil from the pan.

10. Add the sauce, bell peppers, and pineapple pieces to the skillet with the chicken. Gently toss while cooking over low heat.

11. Serve with rice right away.

Chicken Curry

Serves 4-6 people.

Time to Prepare: 10 minutes

Time to cook: 25 minutes

Ingredients

2 tablespoons soy sauce

½ cup water

1 tablespoon sugar

2 tablespoons peanut (or other preferred) oil, divided

2 large yellow onions, cut into thick slices

5 cloves garlic, crushed and minced

1 pound boneless, skinless chicken, cubed

1 ½ tablespoon curry powder

3 medium potatoes, cubed

1 cup fresh or frozen peas

½ teaspoon salt

1 tablespoon cornstarch, blended with enough water to make a thin,

smooth paste

Rice for serving

Directions

1. Combine the soy sauce, water, and sugar in a small bowl.

Set aside after whisking until the sugar is dissolved.

2. Preheat a wok over high heat. Coat the surface with 1 tablespoon of oil. Toss in the onions and garlic for approximately 1-2 minutes, or until the onions begin to soften. Set the onions aside after removing them from the pan.

3. Toss the remaining oil into the pan with the chicken and curry powder, and cook for 4 minutes.

4. Pour in the soy sauce mixture. Combine the potatoes, peas, and onion in a mixing bowl. Season with salt and pepper.

Bring it to a boil for 1 minute, then lower to medium heat, cover, and let simmer for 15 minutes.

5. Remove the cover and stir in the cornstarch and water. Turn the heat up to medium-high. Bring to a boil, stirring constantly, until the sauce thickens.

6. Serve with rice right away.

FISH AND SEAFOOD RECIPES

Lobster-Stuffed Shrimp

2 people

Time to Prepare: 10 minutes

Time to cook: 10 minutes.

Ingredients

2 cups water

4 ounces ground pork

2 tablespoons vegetable oil

1 clove of garlic, minced

10 shrimp, peeled and deveined
148

1 tablespoon rice wine

1 ½ cups chicken or seafood stock

½ teaspoon sesame oil

¼ teaspoon sugar

½ teaspoon salt

Ground white pepper, to taste

½ cup frozen peas

1 small carrot, diced

2 tablespoons cornstarch

2 tablespoons water

1 egg, beaten slightly

1 green onion, chopped for garnish

Directions

1. Bring the water to a boil in a wok or pan. Boil the meat for 1 minute, breaking up any lumps. When the pork is no longer pink, pour it through a sieve and rapidly rinse it.

2. Heat the wok over medium heat once it has been dried. Sauté the garlic in the oil until fragrant. Stir-fry the pork and shrimp for 20 seconds.

3. Cook for 10 seconds longer after adding the wine.

149

4. Combine the chicken stock, sesame oil, sugar, salt, white pepper, peas, and carrots in a mixing bowl.

5. Bring the mixture to a low boil.

6. In a mixing basin, combine cornstarch and water to produce a slurry.

Pour the contents of the wok into it.

7. Allow it to simmer and thicken until it coats the back of a spoon. It may be thinned with water if it becomes too thick.

8. Pour the barely beaten egg into the pan and cook for 5 seconds.

9. Using a spatula, gently fold the egg over.

10. Serve immediately over rice. Garnish with green onions.

Squid with Salt and Pepper

Serves: 4

Time to Prepare: 10 minutes

Time to cook: 7-10 minutes

Ingredients

1 ½ pounds squid, washed, cleaned, cut into uniform bite-size pieces

1 tablespoon rice wine

½ teaspoon sesame oil

Cooking oil for deep-frying

151

½ cup all-purpose flour

½ cup semolina flour

⅓ cup plain cornmeal

1 teaspoon salt, or to taste

White pepper, to taste, preferably freshly-cracked

1 tablespoon cooking or peanut oil or stir-frying

2 teaspoons ginger, minced

5 cloves garlic, sliced

2 long hot green peppers, cut lengthwise and thinly sliced

Cooked rice, for serving

Directions

1. Using paper towels, drain and dry the cleaned, sliced squid.

2. In a mixing dish, combine the wine and sesame oil. For approximately 5 minutes, marinate the squid.

3. In a wok or saucepan, heat the deep-frying oil to 325°F. The oil should be around 4 inches deep.

4. Combine all-purpose flour, semolina flour, cornmeal, salt, and white pepper in a mixing dish and set aside.

5. When the oil is hot enough, carefully squeeze the liquid from the squid and dredge it in the flour mixture.

6. Lower the squid into the oil using a spider strainer or long-handled sieve and cook until golden brown, about 2-3 minutes.

7. Drain the squid on a platter lined with paper towels and season with salt and pepper to taste.

8. Preheat a clean wok on high heat. Add the ginger and a spoonful of oil. Cook until fragrant.

9. Add the garlic and cook until it is faintly yellow.

10. Stir in the peppers for 30 seconds longer.

11. Stir in the squid for 1 minute to cook through and absorb the flavors.

12 Serve immediately over rice.

Kung Pao Shrimp

Serves : 2

Time to Prepare: 10 minutes

Time to cook: 5 minutes

Ingredients

1 pound medium shrimp, peeled and deveined

For marinade

1 tablespoon rice wine

1 teaspoon cornstarch

½ teaspoon salt

For sauce

1 tablespoon sugar

2 tablespoons water

1 tablespoon Chinese black vinegar

1 tablespoon soy sauce

¾ teaspoon cornstarch

½ teaspoon sesame oil

Other ingredients

2 tablespoons vegetable oil

1 large green or red bell pepper, seeds removed and thinly sliced

1 tablespoon garlic, minced

1 tablespoon ginger, peeled and minced

3 Thai chilies, broken in half and seeded

¼ cup chopped unsalted, dry-roasted peanuts

3 cups cooked rice

Directions

1. Combine all of the marinade ingredients and marinate the shrimp for 10 minutes.

2. Combine the sauce ingredients in a mixing bowl. Place aside.

3. Heat the oil in a wok over high heat and swirl it around.

4. Stir-fry the bell pepper, garlic, ginger, and chilies for 1 minute.

5. Stir-fry the shrimp for 2 minutes, or until they have become orange.

6. Stir in the sauce and heat for 30 seconds, or until thickened.

7. Garnish with peanuts and serve over rice.

Spicy Bean Sauce on Fish

4 servings

Preparation 20-minute time limit

Time to cook: 15 minutes

Ingredients

1 large tilapia fillet

For slurry

1 tablespoon water

157

1 tablespoon cornstarch

For sauce

1 tablespoon rice wine

1 tablespoon spicy bean sauce (double)

1 teaspoon hoisin sauce

½ teaspoon sesame oil

½ teaspoon sugar

Ground white pepper

Other ingredients

1-2 tablespoons vegetable or peanut oil, or as needed

1 clove of garlic, minced

¼ cup finely chopped onion

¼ cup ground pork

¼ cup shiitake mushrooms, finely chopped

¼ cup carrot, finely chopped

¼ cup finely chopped red pepper

½ cup water

1 teaspoon sesame oil

Cooked rice, for serving

For garnish

2 teaspoons cilantro, chopped

2 teaspoons green onion, chopped

Directions

1. Steam the fish for 10 minutes in a steamer or on a heatproof plate on a rack over 1 inch of water, covered. When a butter knife easily cuts through the fish to the bottom, it is done.

Remove from the heat and transfer to a serving dish.

2. In a small dish, combine the slurry components and put them aside.

3. Combine all of the sauce ingredients in a mixing bowl and set aside.

4. In a wok, heat the oil over high heat. Cook for a few seconds, until the oil, is aromatic, with the onions and garlic.

5. Combine the pork, mushrooms, carrot, and bell pepper in a mixing bowl. For approximately 1 minute, stir-fry.

6. Add the sauce and water and bring to a boil.

7. Stir in the slurry and continue to simmer until the sauce coats the back of a spoon. If the sauce gets too thick, add more water.

8. Season with sesame oil, remove from heat and drizzle overcooked fish.

9. Garnish with cilantro and green onion and serve immediately over rice.

Black Bean Sauce for Fish

4 servings

Time to Prepare: 5 minutes

Time to cook: 15 minutes.

Ingredients

For the sauce

4 tablespoons black bean sauce

160

1 teaspoon ginger, minced

2 teaspoons garlic powder

3 tablespoons rice wine

1 teaspoon toasted sesame oil

2 tablespoons white sugar

Other ingredients

4 pounds of fish fillets, towel-dried and cut into bite-sized pieces

1 tablespoon cornstarch

5 tablespoons cooking or vegetable oil, divided

1 medium onion, chopped

1 large green bell pepper, seeded and chopped

1 large red bell pepper, seeded and chopped

3 cloves garlic, minced

3 dried red chilies (optional)

Cooked rice, for serving

Directions

1. In a mixing dish, combine all of the sauce ingredients. Place aside.

2. Toss the cornstarch over the fish and put it aside.

3. Melt the butter in a wok over high heat. Add the onion, bell peppers, garlic, and chilies after swirling in the oil (optional). To blend, stir everything together.

4. Pour in 13 cups of the sauce mixture and continue to simmer until the veggies are cooked. Transfer the mixture to a dish using a slotted spoon and set aside.

5. Add 3 tablespoons of oil to the same wok. Add the fish and stir to combine.

6. Pour in the remaining sauce mixture and heat until the fish becomes opaque.

7. Add the veggies back to the wok. Continue to sauté and stir until everything is well heated.

Serve with rice.

Stir-fry Shanghai Shrimp

Serves 4

Time to Prepare: 15 minutes

Time to cook: 10 minutes

Ingredients

1 pound medium shrimp, shelled, deveined, washed, and drained

1 cup oil, for frying

2 green onions, white portion only

3 slices ginger

1 tablespoon rice wine

½ cup chicken broth

1 teaspoon sugar

¼ teaspoon Chinese black vinegar

1 teaspoon sesame oil

Salt, to taste

Directions

1. Using paper towels, pat the shrimp dry.

2. Melt the butter in a wok over high heat. Fry the shrimp for approximately 10 seconds, or until opaque, in the oil. Fry the shrimp in batches to avoid crowding the pot. A spider strainer may be used to lower and hoist the shrimp, as well as to drain the oil back into the wok. Set things aside for now.

3. Heat the oil in the wok nearly to smoking temperature. Lower the shrimp into the oil for a second time and cook for 5-

163

10 seconds. If you fry the shrimp for too long, they will get dry. Take them out of the wok and turn off the heat.

4. Remove any extra oil with a spoon and reheat the oil over low heat.

5. Cook until the green onion whites and ginger are aromatic.

6. Combine the wine, broth, sugar, and vinegar in a mixing bowl. Bring to a simmer and continue to whisk for 30 seconds.

7. Add the sesame oil to the wok with the shrimp. Stir-fry for 5-10 seconds, just long enough to coat the shrimp with the sauce.

8. Season with salt and pepper to taste, and serve.

Scallops in Garlic Sauce with a Spicy

4-6 people

Time to Prepare: 10 minutes

Time to cook: 15 minutes

Ingredients

½ cup chicken broth

1 tablespoon fish sauce

2 teaspoons sherry

1 teaspoon sugar

Peanut (or other preferred) oil

2 green onions, sliced

5 cloves garlic, crushed and minced

1 pound scallops, rinsed and dried

½ cup fresh basil leaves

½ small red bell pepper, diced

1-2 small red hot peppers, sliced

1 tablespoon cornstarch dissolved in enough water to make a thin,

smooth paste

Rice to serve

Directions

1. Combine the chicken broth, fish sauce, sherry, and sugar in a small basin. Stir vigorously until the sugar is fully dissolved. Place aside.

2. Heat the oil in a wok over high heat until it coats the pan.

Toss in the green onions and garlic until aromatic, approximately 1 minute.

3. Gently mix in the prepared scallops, basil leaves, red pepper, and red hot pepper. Cook for around 2-3 minutes.

4. Lower the heat to medium. Stir in the reserved sauce to coat the scallops. Allow the sauce to boil for 4-5 minutes.

Keep a careful eye on the scallops since they may quickly overcook.

5. Push the scallops and veggies to the edges of the wok, leaving the sauce and cooking liquids in the pan.

Stir in the cornstarch mixture to make a smooth sauce.

6. Cook, stirring constantly, until the sauce thickens, approximately 1-2 minutes.

Serve right away over rice.

Cantonese Style Lobster

serves 4-6 people.

Time to prepare: 20 minutes

Time to cook: 20 minutes

Ingredients

2 lobster tails (about 1 pound each)

Salt and pepper to taste

4 cloves garlic, minced

2 tablespoons black bean paste

Peanut (or other preferred) oil, for frying

1-inch piece of ginger, peeled and grated

2 green onions, cut into 1-inch pieces

¼ pound ground pork

1 teaspoon salt

1 cup vegetable or fish stock

2 tablespoons soy sauce

3 tablespoons sherry

1 egg, beaten

1 tablespoon cornstarch, dissolved in enough water to make a thin,

smooth paste

1 green onion for garnish, if desired

Rice for serving

Directions

1. To prepare the lobster, split each tail lengthwise in half. Wash the tails under cold running water, leaving the shells on, and wipe dry with paper towels. Leave the lobster flesh in the shell and chop it into 1-1 12 inch slices. Season to taste with salt and pepper.

2. Mash the minced garlic in a small bowl and stir in the black bean paste. Set aside once you've combined them.

3. Melt the butter in a wok over high heat. Add enough oil to the pan to completely immerse the lobster pieces. When the oil is hot enough, slowly drop the lobster tails into it. Fry the shells until they become reddish. (In this recipe, it is better to utilize the shell color as an indication of doneness.) Make sure the lobster is not overcooked.) Remove the fried lobster tails from the pan and lay them on a platter lined with paper towels to absorb any leftover oil.

4. Allow any residual oil in the pan to cool before discarding all but enough to coat the pan.

5. Add the black bean and garlic combination to the pan and simmer for 1 minute, stirring gently. To prevent additional frying, push the bean paste mixture up the edge of the pan.

6. Combine the ginger, green onions, pork, and salt in a mixing bowl. Cook, tossing slowly, until the meat browns.

7. Pour the stock, soy sauce, and sherry into the pan.

Reintroduce the bean paste mixture after the liquid has warmed up.

Bring the water to a boil.

8. Toss in the cooked lobster tails. Cook for one minute, stirring constantly. Allow the lobster to steam for 3 minutes, covered.

9. Take off the cover and stir in the cornstarch mixture. Season to taste. Pour in the beaten egg slowly, swirling it around until it is cooked.

10. Remove from the heat and, if wanted, garnish with green onion. Serve with rice right away.

Moo Shu Shrimp serves 4-6 people.

Time to Prepare: 30 minutes

Time to cook: 15 minutes

Ingredients

Mu Shu pancakes

2 cups flour

¾ cup water, boiling

2 tablespoons sesame oil

Shrimp filling

2 teaspoons cornstarch

1 teaspoon chili garlic sauce

2 tablespoons soy sauce

1 tablespoon hoisin sauce

1 tablespoon peanut (or other preferred) oil

1 pound small shrimp, peeled and deveined

5 cloves garlic, crushed and minced

2 cups shiitake mushrooms, sliced

3 green onions, sliced, with greens and whites separated

1 medium carrot, shredded

1 small head of napa cabbage, shredded

Directions

Pancakes Mu Shu

1. In a mixing bowl, gently whisk boiling water into the flour to form the Mu Shu pancakes. Mix with a fork until a soft dough forms. Turn the dough out onto a floured surface and knead it until stiff and elastic. Cover and set aside for 20 minutes.

2. Roll the dough into a log about a foot long. Cut it into 1-inch pieces and shape each one into a little ball.

3. Using your hand, flatten each ball and brush with sesame oil.

Using a rolling pin, flatten each pancake until it is approximately 6 inches wide.

4. Cook the pancakes, one at a time, in a medium nonstick skillet over medium heat until they are faintly golden brown on the edges, approximately 1-2 minutes on each side.

5 Wrap them in foil and put them aside.

Filling made with shrimp

6. In a small bowl, whisk together the cornstarch and water to produce a thin, clump-free paste. To the bowl, combine the chili garlic sauce, soy sauce, and hoisin sauce. Whisk until the mixture is well combined. Place aside.

7. Melt the butter in a wok over high heat. Coat the pan with oil. Toss the shrimp and garlic in the pan carefully. Cook for 2-3 minutes, or until the shrimp are pink and fully cooked. Place them on a chopping board after removing them from the pan. Chop each shrimp into 4-6 pieces and set aside.

8. If necessary, add extra oil to the wok. Add the mushrooms, onions, and carrots once the oil is hot. Cook for 3-4 minutes, stirring gently. Cook until the cabbage is barely wilted, approximately 2-3 minutes, in the vegetable mixture.

9. Return the shrimp pieces to the wok.

10. Gently whisk in the prepared cornstarch mixture to coat.

Stir-fry the shrimp and sauce for approximately 1 minute to warm them up.

11. Serve with Mu Shu Pancakes right away.

Lake Tung Ting Shrimp

serves 4 people.

Time to prepare: 20 minutes, plus 30-60 minutes of marinating time

Time to cook: 25 minutes

Ingredients

2 tablespoons soy sauce

½ cup sherry or dry white wine

¼ cup water plus cooking water

1 teaspoon cornstarch

174

1 pound large shrimp, peeled and deveined (shells reserved)

1 tablespoon peanut (or other preferred) oil

2 cups broccoli florets

1 medium carrot, sliced diagonally

1 celery stalk, sliced diagonally

1 cup green beans, washed and trimmed

1 cup snow peas, washed and trimmed

4 cloves garlic, crushed and minced

1 1-inch piece of ginger, peeled and grated

1 bunch of green onions, greens reserved for garnish

¼ cup fish stock

Rice for serving

Directions

1. Combine the soy sauce, sherry, 14 cups of water, and cornstarch in a medium mixing bowl. Whisk until thoroughly combined and free of clumps. Toss the

175

shrimp in the basin to coat them. Refrigerate for 30-60 minutes with the lid on.

2. Put the shrimp shells in a small saucepan and cover with just enough water to cover. Simmer on low heat while the shrimp marinates in the fridge. The liquid in the pan will evaporate, yielding a delicious broth. Set aside after draining and discarding the shells.

3. Melt the butter in a wok over medium-high heat. Pour in just enough oil to coat the pan. Combine the broccoli, carrots, celery, green beans, and snow peas in a large mixing bowl. Cook, turning gently, for 4-5 minutes, or until the veggies are crisp and vivid in color. Stir in the garlic, ginger, and green onions, and continue to stir-fry for another minute.

4. Take the shrimp out of the refrigerator and place it in the pan.

Toss to combine and cook for 1 minute. Combine the remaining marinade, fish sauce, and shell stock in a mixing bowl. Bring to a boil after completely mixing. Stir the sauce until it thickens. The shrimp should be cooked completely and the color should have changed.

5. Remove from the heat and immediately serve over rice.

If desired, garnish with green onions.

VEGETARIAN RECIPES

Vegetables in a Variety

2 people

Time to prepare: 10 minutes

Time to cook: 8 minutes

Ingredients

For thickener (slurry)

2 ½ teaspoons cornstarch

1 tablespoon water

For stir-fry

177

1 tablespoon vegetable oil

1 clove of garlic, minced

1 small red pepper, sliced

1 small carrot, sliced

4 mushrooms, sliced

½ cup bamboo shoots

½ cup water chestnuts

1 cup broccoli florets

½ cup vegetable stock

Salt, to taste

2 teaspoons soy sauce

Directions

1. Whisk together the thickening ingredients. Place aside.

2. In a wok, heat the oil over high heat. Stir in the garlic until it is aromatic.

3. Combine the red bell pepper, carrots, mushrooms, bamboo shoots, and water chestnuts in a mixing bowl. 1 minute of stirring

4. Stir in the bean sprouts for 2 minutes.

5. Add the veggie broth and bring to a boil.

6. Before putting the thickener into the pan, give it a short swirl.

Stir until the sauce thickens.

7. Season with salt and soy sauce, then adjust to taste.

8. Serve while still hot.

4 Servings of Egg Foo Yung

Time to Prepare: 30 minutes

Time to cook: 20 minutes

Ingredients

3 tablespoons peanut oil, or as needed

Rice for serving

For omelet

6 eggs, beaten

1 cup bean sprouts

¼ cup green onions, minced

180

¼ cup Chinese cabbage, shredded

4 water chestnuts, minced

½ cup ground vegetarian meat substitute or tofu, chopped

1 teaspoon soy sauce

For thickener

1 tablespoon cornstarch

2 tablespoons water

For Sauce

1 cup vegetable broth

1 tablespoon soy sauce

2 teaspoons sugar

2 teaspoons vinegar

Rice for serving

181

Directions

1. Combine the omelet ingredients in a mixing basin. Combine thoroughly.

2. Preheat a wok over medium heat. Swirl the oil around.

3. Scoop up approximately 13 cups of the egg mixture and sprinkle it about the pan in a circular motion.

4. When the bottom is golden brown, turn it over to brown the other side.

Place it on a platter.

5. Stir the egg mixture and create another omelet.

Repeat until all of the omelet mixtures has been utilized.

6. To prepare a thickening, combine the cornstarch and water.

7. In a saucepan, combine the sauce ingredients. Bring it to a boil and then reduce to low heat.

8. Stir in the thickening and cook until it is thick enough to coat the back of a spoon.

9th. Serve with an omelet (egg foo young). The sauce may be poured over the omelet or served separately in a dish. To serve, place the omelet on top of the rice.

Green Beans Sautéed in a Dry Sauce

4 servings

Time to Prepare: 5 minutes

Time to cook: 10 minutes

Ingredients

2 tablespoons peanut oil for stir-frying, or as needed

1 pound Chinese long beans, trimmed and cut into 3-inch pieces

1 tablespoon garlic, chopped

1 tablespoon ginger, chopped

2 green onions, white parts only, finely chopped

½ teaspoon chili paste

1 tablespoon dark soy sauce

½ teaspoon sugar

Salt and pepper, to taste

Sesame seeds for garnish

Directions

1. Melt the butter in a wok over medium heat. 1 tablespoon oil, swirled in

2. Add the beans and stir-fry for 7 minutes, or until they shrivel and become slightly browned, before removing to drain on paper towels. Place aside.

3. Increase the heat to high and add another tablespoon of oil to the pan.

4. Cook until the garlic, ginger, and green onions are aromatic.

5. Stir in the chili paste to unleash the scent.

6. Return the beans to the skillet and add the soy sauce, sugar, salt, and pepper to taste.

7. Stir in the ingredients and adjust to taste.

8. Garnish with sesame seeds and serve right away.

Tofu with Salt & Pepper Serves: 2-4

Time to Prepare: 10 minutes

Time to cook: 10 minutes

Ingredients

For tofu

1 14-ounce block of extra firm tofu, drained

4 tablespoons cornstarch

Salt and pepper

Vegetable or peanut oil for frying

For stir-fry

1 tablespoon vegetable or peanut oil

1 cup leeks, white parts only, chopped

½ cup celery, chopped

½ cup green pepper, chopped

1 tablespoon garlic, minced

1 tablespoon ginger, minced

1 tablespoon light soy sauce

½ teaspoon brown sugar

For garnish

Green onions, chopped

Chili sauce

Directions

1. In a medium mixing bowl, combine the cornstarch, salt, and pepper.

2. Using paper towels, pat the tofu dry and cut it into cubes.

187

3. Toss the tofu cubes in the cornstarch mixture, being careful to fully coat each cube.

4. In a wok, heat the oil over high heat. Allow the oil to heat up to a depth of 12 inches.

5. Fry the cubes in batches; if the pan is too crowded, the tofu will not be crispy. To ensure that both sides are golden brown, flip the pan.

6. Pat the tofu dry with paper towels.

7. Melt the butter in a clean wok over medium-high heat. Stir-fry the leeks, celery, and green pepper for 2 minutes in 1 tbsp oil.

8. Stir in the ginger and garlic for another 2 minutes.

9. Stir in the soy sauce and brown sugar and cook for another 30 seconds before adding the tofu cubes and tossing thoroughly.

10. Garnish with green onions and serve with a side of chili sauce.

Mapo Tofu

servings :3-4

Time to Prepare: 5 minutes

Time to cook: 15 minutes

Ingredients

For thickener

½ cup chicken or vegetable broth

1 teaspoon cornstarch

2 teaspoons soy sauce

189

1 teaspoon sugar

For stir-fry

1 tablespoon sesame oil

2 cloves garlic, minced

2 teaspoons ginger, minced

4 green onions, white part only, minced

1 tablespoon fermented black beans, roughly chopped

½ teaspoon Sichuan peppercorns, black seeds removed, ground

6 ounces vegetarian ground meat substitute*

2 teaspoons chili bean paste

1 14-ounce block of silken tofu, drained and cut into ¾-inch cubes

For garnish

Green onions, green part only, minced

Directions

1. Combine the thickening ingredients in a mixing dish. Set aside.

2. In a wok, heat the sesame oil over high heat. Garlic, ginger, and green onions should be stir-fried until aromatic.

3. Combine the black beans and Sichuan pepper in a mixing bowl. For a few seconds, stir.

4. Stir in the ground pork, breaking up any lumps.

Cook, stirring occasionally until the meat is browned.

5. Stir in the chili bean paste until completely combined.

6. Toss in the tofu chunks, being careful not to crush them.

7. Stir in the thickener and add it to the wok.

8. Bring the sauce to a boil by stirring the contents of the pan.

Remove the wok from the heat after the sauce has thickened.

9. Serve over rice and garnished with green onion.

* To make it non-vegetarian, add ground pork instead of ground beef.

Garlic-Spiced Chinese Eggplant

4 servings

Time to Prepare: 15 minutes

Time to cook: 15 minutes

Ingredients

1 tablespoon peanut oil

5 Asian eggplants, cut into 1-inch wedges

1 1-inch piece fresh ginger, peeled and grated
192

3 cloves garlic, minced and crushed

1 fresh red chili, sliced

2 green onions, sliced with white and green parts separated

3 tablespoons soy sauce

1 ½ tablespoons brown sugar

1 tablespoon sesame oil

2 tablespoons rice vinegar

1 tablespoon cornstarch

½ cup vegetable broth

Toasted sesame seeds for garnish (optional)

Thai holy basil for garnish (optional)

Rice for serving

Directions

1. Heat a wok over high heat and coat the pan evenly with peanut oil.

2. Add a single layer of eggplant to the heated wok. Cook for 2-3 minutes, stirring gently. Depending

on the size of your wok, you may need to cook the eggplant in batches.

3. When the eggplant is done, take it from the skillet and put it aside.

4. Return a tiny quantity of peanut oil to the wok. Combine the ginger, garlic, chile, and white sections of the green onions in a mixing bowl.

Cook, swirling gently, for about 2 minutes, or until the ingredients begin to emit a strong scent.

5. Combine the soy sauce, brown sugar, sesame oil, vinegar, and cornstarch in a small basin. Whisk until completely combined and free of cornstarch clumps.

6. Add the stock and soy sauce combination to the pan and simmer for two minutes, or until the sauce has thickened somewhat.

7. Return the eggplant to the pan and stir to coat.

8. Serve immediately with rice and, if wanted, sprinkle with sesame seeds and basil.

Hunan Bean Curd

4 servings

Time to Prepare: 15 minutes

Time to cook: 20 minutes

Ingredients

1 tablespoon peanut (or other preferred) oil

1 ½ 14-ounce blocks of extra firm tofu, cubed

2 cups broccoli florets

1 teaspoon chili bean paste

2 teaspoons crushed red pepper

195

1 cup shiitake or any Asian mushrooms, cut into large pieces

3 cloves garlic, crushed and minced

1 cup vegetable stock

½ teaspoon soy sauce

2 teaspoons sherry

1 teaspoon sesame oil

½ teaspoon cornstarch, mixed with enough water to form a thin

paste

½ teaspoon salt

Green onions for garnish (optional)

Rice for serving

Directions

1. Heat a wok over high heat and add enough oil to coat the pan gently.

2. Add the tofu to the heated pan and stir constantly until it starts to brown. Set the tofu aside after removing it from the pan.

3. To the wok, add the broccoli, bean paste, and crushed red pepper. Cook for approximately 2 minutes, stirring gently.

4. Cook for one minute after adding the mushrooms and garlic before adding the vegetable stock.

5. Place the tofu back in the pan. Combine the soy sauce, sherry, and sesame oil in a mixing bowl. 1 minute in the oven

6. Stir in the cornstarch mixture and boil for 3 minutes, or until the sauce thickens. If desired, season with salt.

Serve immediately with rice and, if wanted, garnish with green onions.

Vegetables of Green Jade

4-6 people

Time to Prepare: 15 minutes

Time to cook: 15 minutes

Ingredients

2 cups mini bok choy, rinsed and trimmed

3 cups broccoli, chopped, including stems

1 teaspoon sugar

½ cup water

4 tablespoons low-sodium soy sauce

½ tablespoon sesame oil

1 tablespoon cornstarch

2 tablespoons peanut (or other preferred) oil

1 onion, diced

2 cloves garlic, crushed and minced

1 1-inch piece of fresh ginger, peeled and grated

2 cups snow peas, rinsed and trimmed

3 tablespoons rice wine vinegar

½ teaspoon salt

Rice for serving

Directions

1. Blanch the bok choy and broccoli for 2 minutes in a large saucepan filled with boiling water. To halt the cooking process, drain and rinse with cold water. Place aside.

2. Combine the sugar, water, soy sauce, sesame oil, and cornstarch in a small mixing dish. Place aside.

3. Heat 1 or 2 tablespoons of peanut oil in a wok over medium-high heat. Combine the onion, garlic, and ginger in a mixing bowl. 1 minute in the oven

4. Combine the broccoli, bok choy, and snow peas in a large mixing bowl. Cook, turning gently, for 3-4 minutes, or until the veggies soften slightly and brighten in color.

5. Add the rice wine vinegar and cover to allow the veggies to simmer and absorb the wine flavor. 1 minute in the oven

6. Stir in the soy sauce mixture, then add it to the pan and simmer just until the sauce thickens. If preferred, season with salt and serve immediately with rice.

RECIPES FOR DESSERT

Fortune cookies

36 servings

Time to Prepare: 15 minutes

Time to cook: 10 minutes

Ingredients

3 egg whites

¾ cup white sugar

201

½ cup butter, melted and cooled

¼ teaspoon vanilla extract

¼ teaspoon almond extract

1 cup all-purpose flour

2 tablespoons water

Directions

1. Make fortunes out of strips of paper.

2. Preheat the oven to 375 degrees Fahrenheit.

3. Line a cookie sheet with parchment paper or spray with nonstick cooking spray.

4. Whip the egg whites and sugar with an electric mixer on high speed for approximately 2 minutes, or until frothy.

5. Mix in the melted butter, vanilla, almond extract, flour, and water on low speed.

6. Spoon the batter in 3-inch circles onto the cookie sheets.

Repeat until all of the batters has been used up. Make sure there is adequate space between the rings.

7. Bake for 5-7 minutes, or until the edges start to become golden brown.

If you overbake them, they will become too rigid to fold. If you underbake them, they will have a spongy feel.

8. Quickly draw a circle, center the fortune strip, then fold the biscuit in half over the fortune.

9. Make a horseshoe form by folding the ends together.

10. Set aside to cool and set. You may place them in muffin tins to keep them from popping open.

Pudding with Mango

8 servings

Setting time: 3 hours

Preparation time: 3 hours

Time to cook: 15 minutes

Ingredients

2 tablespoons/envelopes unflavored gelatin

¾ cup sugar

1 cup hot water

3 cups fresh mangoes, pureed

1 cup evaporated milk

8 ice cubes

Whipped cream and fresh mango slices or cubes for garnish

Directions

1. In a small bowl, dissolve the gelatin and sugar in boiling water. Check for any lumps or undissolved gelatin.

2. In a large mixing bowl, combine the mango puree, evaporated milk, and ice cubes.

3. While stirring, pour the mango mixture into the gelatin mixture.

Stir the mixture until the ice cubes have melted.

4. Pour into molds and place in the refrigerator to set (about 3 hours).

5. When the mold has firm, remove the sides with a butter knife and flip it onto a serving plate. You may also release the mold by temporarily immersing it in hot water.

6. Serve with whipped cream and mango segments as garnish.

Cookies with Almonds

60 cookies are made.

Time to prepare: 10 minutes + 2 hours cooling time

Time to cook: 15 minutes

Ingredients

2 ½ cups all-purpose flour, sifted

½ teaspoon baking soda

½ teaspoon salt

½ pound butter

1 cup white sugar

1 large egg, lightly beaten

2 teaspoons almond extract

½ teaspoon vanilla extract

60 blanched almonds for garnish (optional)

Directions

1. Combine the flour, baking soda, and salt in a large mixing basin.

2. In a separate dish, cream the butter with an electric mixer until it is smooth. Mix in the sugar well. Mix in the egg and extract until well combined.

3. In four equal increments, add the dry ingredients to the creamed butter and sugar, fully mixing

after each one. After combining, the dough will be coarse and crumbly. Form the dough into two compact balls and cover with plastic wrap. Refrigerate for at least 30 minutes before serving. The dough may also be frozen and used later.

Preheat the oven to 350°F.

5. Remove the dough from the refrigerator when ready to bake the cookies. Form little 1-inch balls with your hands and lay them on a baking sheet lined with parchment paper, allowing approximately an inch between cookies. Fill each biscuit with a blanched almond and flatten the edges.

6. Bake the cookies in batches for 12-15 minutes, or until the edges are softly golden brown and aromatic.

7. Set aside to cool before serving.

Doughnuts from China

12 servings

Time to Prepare: 15 minutes

Time to cook: 10 minutes

Ingredients

2 cups all-purpose flour

2 ½ teaspoons baking powder

½ teaspoon salt

⅓ cup butter, cubed

¾ cup milk

209

Oil for frying

Granulated sugar for dusting

Directions

1. Combine the flour, baking powder, and salt in a medium-sized mixing basin.

2. Using your hands, combine the butter into the flour mixture until it is crumbly but not clumpy.

3. Stir in the milk until a hard dough forms.

4. Place the dough on a lightly floured work area and knead until it forms an elastic ball. At this point, avoid over-kneading the dough.

5. Heat 2 inches of oil in a wok or skillet big enough for frying over medium-high heat.

6. Roll the dough into golf ball-sized balls. Apply gentle pressure to flatten somewhat.

7. Fry the doughnuts in small batches, taking care not to overcrowd the pan.

Slowly drop them into the oil and cook for 4 minutes, flipping once, until golden brown.

8. Take the doughnuts out of the oil and sprinkle them with sugar.

9. Let them cool somewhat before serving.

CONCLUSION

Takeout Chinese is a significant aspect of American history and culture.

Cooking the recipes in this book allows you to participate in America's cultural legacy. Although you won't have the convenience of having it delivered to your home, cooking your own Chinese takeout-inspired meals will be a one-of-a-kind experience as well as a chance to create nutritious food for yourself and your family.

Have fun on your journey.